Hobbies

COIN   collecting
STAMP   "
Wood Carving "
Rocks   "
Stock Investing
STAINED GLASS —
Pyro.
Wood CARVING
CAR BUILD/MAINT.
Photography
Gold Prospecting/Rock Col.
COMPUTER

EXERCISE

Ti Chi
WALK/Hike
Bike Riding
SWIM   Weights
DANCE   Ex. Bike
BOWL
Golf
KAYACK
Fishing   beach, lake, stream

Social

SIRS
EBMUD Ret.
Stock Club
Bowl
Dance
Moose Club
Family
Sr Housing Active Adult
CARDS

Yacation Spots.

Alaska	Wash. DC	ARIZONA
HAWAii	Penn.	MONTANA
CANCOUN	NEW OrleAns	Yellowstone
MAZATLAN	LoS UAyes	OREGON/WASH
B.C. Victoria	Death Valley	San Diego

weekend get AWAys

FortuNA	SAntA Barb.
Redwoods	Yosemite
Taho	SAn Francisco
Pt Rayes	
JenneR	

WORK

Consultant Inspector
TEACHing MATH 6-9 grade
DRAFTING Arch.
Habitat for Humanity
Build House
 "   CAR
Restore Enviroment - Trails, Dino Dig
Yard work.

How to Create Your Own Super Second Life

What Are You Going to Do With Your Extra 30 Years?

Gordon Burgett

Communication **U**nlimited

Santa Maria, California

ISBN 0-910167-60-5

Disclaimer: This book is designed to provide information in regard to the subject matter covered. It is sold with the understanding that the publisher and author are not engaged in rendering legal, medical, financial, or other professional services. If such expert assistance is desired or required, the services of a competent professional should be sought.

Published by Communication Unlimited, P.O. Box 6405, Santa Maria, CA 93456 / (800) 563-1454. Other fine Communication Unlimited publications are available from your bookstore or directly from the publisher. See related information on the last two pages of this book or check http://www.agemasters.com or www.sops.com.

ACKNOWLEDGMENTS

The world is full of productive, vibrant Super Second Lifers. I've been fortunate to have among my friends many models of how a second life should be lived, though they will shudder to see their names in print for doing nothing more than being vital, good, loving people. I'm thinking of Lu Hintz, whose days are spent trying to birdie the sixteenth hole while at night he sings in quartets, creates a newsletter, and teaches English to immigrants—and his wife, Mary, who is even busier! Of Helen Myers, who volunteers at the hospital, gardens, golfs, travels, and decided, on a whim, to sky dive at 79. I'm thinking of Cy, Wally, Jim, Larry, Glenn, Katherine Stackpoole, my N.S.A. Gold Coast comrades, my brothers Bill and Jim, many fellow warblers, and a dozen others who have come into their own as they age and are making the world better because of their wisdom and efficacy. They don't need my book. They're just figuring it out themselves.

Conversely, my heart goes out to others who seem to unplug at about 55 or 60. I feel helpless in their presence. That's one reason I'm writing this book. It's a way I know to help them—and myself, who is suddenly their age and never thought much about either a first or second life, until the first was almost over and the second arrived, unbeckoned.

Particular thanks go to Kim Wolinski, Eileen Gold, and Mary Hintz (again), who read this tome in the rough—it, not them—and set me straight, then to Linda Lange, who got the last chance to pick through it, lovingly, near its completion. If errors or inanity still survived and reached print, it's despite their best efforts!

There's little worse than having a boss who also writes because the staff must then pick up the slack while trying to ignore his random musings and vacuous stares. Nobody will be happier to see these pages in print and orders flying in the door! A giant hug to Linda (again), Robyn, Melinda, and Wally (again).

I'm wrong. There is one person who will be even happier to see others sharing these words: Marsha (Freeman), my wife. Widowed again to that sultry seductress, the laptop (nee the pen)! Fortunately, she loves the concept and has been the book's strongest champion.

DEDICATION

To Ray Crowley, who passed at 83 as these pages went to press. Ray is my father-in-law, a gentle man who played a mean racquetball and probably taught half of Tulsa how to swim at the Y. Ray enjoyed every minute of his extra 30 years.

GORDON BURGETT

◆ In 1999, Gordon Burgett wrote *How to Create Your Own Super Second Life: What Are You Going to Do With Your Extra 30 Years?* He currently speaks nationwide about this topic, offering keynotes, break-out sessions, and workshops at conventions, group meetings, retreats, and at universities.

◆ Since 1981, Burgett has also published 1,600+ articles and offered an average of 100 seminars and speeches annually, mostly to dental and medical associations, conventions nationwide, and through university extension programs. During that time he has appeared extensively on radio and TV, as a guest author and a publishing specialist. Burgett is a long-standing member of the National Speakers Association, the American Society of Authors and Journalists, and the Publishers Marketing Association; has produced 26 audio cassette series and singles, and has published 18 books, including:

❖ *Sell and Resell Your Magazine Articles*
❖ *Standard Marketing Procedures for Dentists*
❖ *Publishing to Niche Markets*
❖ *Treasure and Scavenger Hunts*
❖ *Niche Marketing for Writers, Speakers, and Entrepreneurs*
❖ *Self-Publishing to Tightly-Targeted Markets*
❖ *The Travel Writer's Guide*

❖ *How to Sell More Than 75% of Your Freelance Writing*
❖ *The Writer's Guide to Query and Cover Letters*
❖ *Empire-Building by Writing and Speaking*
❖ *Speaking for Money (with Mike Frank)*
❖ *Ten Sales from One Article Idea*
❖ *The Query Book*

◆ Four of Burgett's books have been Writer's Digest Book Club top choices: *Sell and Resell Your Magazine Articles, The Travel Writer's Guide, The Writer's Guide to Query and Cover Letters,* and *How to Sell More Than 75% of Your Freelance Writing.*

◆ Gordon has owned and directed a publishing company, Communication Unlimited, since 1981. It specializes in books, reports, and cassettes about writing, empire-building, and niche publishing. In 1995, the company merged with Marsha Freeman's Team Systems and created Dental Communication Unlimited and Medical Communication Unlimited, to begin a series of standard operating procedures manuals (and other, related office operations products) for health care professionals. (See *www.sops.com.*)

◆ Burgett earned four academic degrees: B.A., University of Illinois, Champaign-Urbana (Latin American Studies), M.A., University of Wisconsin, Madison (Luso-Brazilian Studies), M.F.T. Thunderbird Graduate School (Foreign Trade), and an M.A., Northern Illinois University (U.S. Intellectual History). He was twice an university dean, taught Portuguese and history, created a city recreation program in Illinois, directed CARE (and Peace Corps) programs in Colombia and Ecuador (including the Land Directorship of the HOPE ship medical/dental program in Guayaquil), twice studied in Brazil, played professional baseball, and led a gold hunt up the Paushi Yaco (Upper Amazon) River in Ecuador.

◆ Gordon is also the creator of Age Masters, an Internet acknowledgment and listing service for athletic achievements in running, walking, cycling, swimming and wheeling. (See *www.agemasters.com.*)

For further information, call (805) 937-8711 or see www.agemasters.com.

CONTENTS

Introduction

PART ONE   Getting Ready for Your Super Second Life

PART TWO   Planning, Implementing, and Living Your Super Second Life

---

GRAPHS, CHARTS, WORKSHEETS

Part One

Getting Ready
for Your
Super Second Life

Introduction

An absurd idea...

When I was ten, a book like this would have seemed absurd. That was 1948 and mostly I remember two things—a loud neighborhood party when the war ended (we were supposedly sound asleep several doors away) and my mother crying when Franklin Delano Roosevelt died.

And during my earlier years, say 20 to 40, I was too busy just surviving and doing what everybody else did to give it much thought. My only sense of mortality was one night, at 38, realizing that I would no longer get that desperate call from the Cubs to put on the gear, get behind the plate, and bring them a pennant. Old age and death seemed a million years away.

The crack in my immortality came when I was 50, the year my 27-year marriage hit the shoals while our girls were in Europe celebrating their college degrees. Suddenly the future seemed endless. I'd never thought about retirement, hobbies, or later-life goals. The infinite was finite. If I could work forever I could live forever. I needed this book then, but it didn't exist.

Blame the "Boomers"!

That it does exist you can blame on the "boomers"—if you're into blaming. It took their reaching 50 to provide much public focus on a sensible, rewarding older age.

What put my pen in this pasture was a chance remark on the radio, something about our current life expectancy and the 50-80 later-life vacuum being just as long as the maturing bubble for those 20-50.

Then just about everything I heard or read for the next two weeks seemed to be about retirement and nobody being prepared—like me. Was that true? I love research, I'm a writer, and the line was drawn.

What do we most need to know about retirement?
How can we prepare to live happily into the unknown?
How can we be in control of our own actions and fate?
What do we do first?

What I found is on these pages. I was sixty when I started this book. One of those things was that a whole lot of us sexagenarians never heard the phrase "Super Second Life." But we're not alone. Those noisy, puffing boomers, bless them, hadn't either (beyond chucking money into their 401k's), and anyone younger, I might as well be writing about corset hooks or one-horse shays. (Alas, their day will come...)

A last thought. I could have moaned for 240 pages about our lack of preparation. Or listed 700 or 7,000 ways to get ready. But why? Who wants to read that? What I really want to know is summed up in two questions:

The book answers these two questions

(1) What is a "Super Second Life" and how might we be better and happier by creating our own? and
(2) Specifically, what can we do now to prepare ourselves to live each of the days that we have left to its fullest?

The answers are found in Parts One and Two.

This book is a reference guide, a blueprint, and a map all in one. Please take its words and process and from them create your own wildly worthwhile, exciting, envious Super Second Life.

Enough introduction

Enough babbling. Neither of us are getting any younger. Let me find my specs and let's get going...

What Are You Going to Do With Your Extra 30 Years?

1

So you're 40 or 50, big deal. The only question that counts is "What are you going to do with your next 30 years?"

Nobody in the history of man has lived as long as you—and ended up in such good shape.

Your ancestors had kids, but rarely saw their kids have kids. Most women never knew menopause. Men died when their legs, eyes, or ears failed.

In 1900, the average life expectancy was 48. Now it's 78, only a hundred years later. For most, 30 extra years! What a wonderful problem!

So here you are, feeling fine, looking good, full of ginger, all bucketed up and historically with no place to go.

You might as well make a plan that will use all your knowledge and experience, your values and laughter, in those "new" 30 years.

Your parents, certainly theirs, subscribed to the "declining philosophy" that said that from midlife on it was all downhill, that the party was over, dreams unrealized were just that. But today that's as out of date as your prom dress, ball glove, or 8-tracks. People now don't just curl up and die when they hit the 50-yard line. In fact, most bloom like never before. Better yet, they have the skill, strength, wisdom, and experience—sometimes even the money—to make their second half the joyous completion of what the first half prepared them to do.

Of course, whether that happens to you is pretty much your choice. Just sitting around waiting to die can take a long time, if curling up is your thing...

3

You at least deserve some options to use in the time in between. Plenty of books tell you to save billions for your "retirement." Others urge you to volunteer 26 hours a day. But none shows you how to take your future by the reins and make it go precisely where you wish.

This book has that goal: to help you plan the rest of your days.

You can use it to map out the great unknown—your Super Second Life!

Then you will have 100 options, and a hundred alternatives, and maybe 100 new friends.

What the book is all about.

Extra years...

Of all the people who *ever* reached 65 years of age, one half of them are alive today!

If you lived to half that age during the Dark Ages, you were very, very old. Living too many years has hardly been a historical problem!

The miracle is that most of us will live into our 80s, and some far beyond 100. We may even know a person who will live to 200.

How valuable are those extra years? They're only worth having if they are worth living.

No strings attached

We get 30 more years just for being alive at the end of a century rather than at the start—a gift with no strings attached!

That's how much life expectancy has increased since 1900. Years to do with as we wish. We *all* get them, or at least the chance at them.

But who reading these pages has a plan for them? We didn't plan our first life, and when we hit the 40s and early 50s, when the gift kicks in, we have no plan for the extra years either.

I'm not scolding. I'm 61 and never gave a thought to any of this: extra years, a plan, a gift-horse, until I saw that life expectancy in 1900 and that my grandmothers lived to about 90, and it hit me that I'm spending my gift without even knowing that I'd gotten it. Just frittering it away, for the most part.

Yet if you and I had a plan we could take this gift, this jewel, and cut it and set it ourselves and make it shine. If we considered these extra 30 years our second life, our gift life, we could finally do what we wanted to do by intent, free from the toil and expectations and often the sheer nonsense of our first life.

Thirty free years. A gift horse. With a plan, that's found gold.

All we need is an Action Plan

So let me help you, and me, do that. Let's start creating Action Plans for our own Super Second Lives.

This book, then, is not about "retirement." Most of us reading it will not retire in the way our parents did (and the government wanted, so we would open up jobs for the young). We won't be throwing down our hod or rug beaters at 65, bent and shot.

When the "Iron Chancellor" Otto von Bismarck, in the late 1800s, plucked a retirement age of 70 out of the air, thinking it so old that the German state would hardly have to pay pensions at all, it was far beyond the average life expectancy.

"Old age is when it's not so hard to avoid temptation as it is to find it."

Cosmo Sardo

When F.D.R. created an old-age retirement system in the United States, and lowered it to 65, it still was. Today, a person 65 will probably be line dancing two decades later.

Nor is this book solely directed to the 40 plus. In truth, it should be mandatory reading in high school, or college at the latest, so the readers could plan both their first *and* second lives—and make each super.

But that will never happen. Kids in their late teens and 20s are too juicy and jumpy, invincible, and all-knowing. They might agree that there's a kernel of truth to what these pages say but they'd consider it about as applicable as a Byzantine grunt.

The best time to start planning?

This is a book designed to help you use your gift to its fullest by creating your own Super Second Life. That's when the very best living takes place, or can. But for that to be so requires thought, some planning, decisions made, and some dreams dreamed and action acted.

So I chose 40 as an arbitrary time to start planning and suspect that most of the readers will tune in between then and 55, an age when thinking about going backwards to become a kid again makes your fewer hairs stand straight up in horror. You've outgrown that posturing and madness. Anyway, nature won't let you.

The problem is what you think you see ahead: less power, less beauty, less passion, less money, and less years.

You need better eyes. The truth is, the second half of your life will be better, more exciting, and much more in your control than the hard half you're escaping.

You're in midlife, and as soon as you stop yelling "Crisis!" and waltz through it, you're going to pop out a new, calmer, stronger person.

And since you had the wisdom to buy a book telling you how to create a "Super Second Life," not only are you going to be ready to leap into your new body and mind to enjoy your second journey, you're also going to be able to extract every last drop of joy from it.

Part Two
of this book

In the second half of this book I'll walk you, step-by-step, through a straightforward process of planning, then implementing, for those years. It starts with a Dream List and ends with a detailed Action Plan for the coming stages of your life. (If your dream machine has gotten rusty, I'll even share 200 rather generic dreams in the Appendix that you can pick from.)

But in this half let's talk about that dreaded "midlife crisis," nature, liberation, what you did right, and what you want to shuck as soon as you can. Then we'll discuss the business of staying healthy and a different look at staying solvent, before we figure out how to spend that vigor and cash!

Why plan at all?
Why not just
let it happen?

The best answer may be that since you didn't plan for the first half and you've only got the second half left, do you want to be planless your entire life?

I know, you did plan the first half—without my book.

Malarkey. You've been led around by the hormones for most of the last 40 years, and when they didn't drag you from school to marriage to babies, and beauty and brawn to jobs and success (all in the name of sex, and maybe love), then society kicked in and picked the order and the rituals while delineating the restraints. Don't fret: nature and society enslaved us all, and it wasn't so bad. We've paid our reproductive dues, have kids we love, and, despite ourselves half the time, built up a kitbag of knowledge and skills. We even pocketed some coins and slipped in some fun.

Sure, you chose your spouse, picked your job, and have been in control of every facet of your life from the time you were six. Yep, and there's a gold bar on the back of this book.

See Chapter 4 for more about those early years and what we will gladly leave behind.

The point is: whatever the past, you survived it and came out ahead.

Now you've got 30 more years and this time you *are* in charge. So why not take all those street smarts, school learning, and people skills and put them to full use to design the kind of life you want, then make that happen?

In Chapter 8 you will be asked a simple question: "If you had all the money, time, and energy you needed and were free from any outside constraints, what would you do in your extra 30 years?" From the answers, you create your own Dream List. What's left is the defining and doing.

It's your life and your last days. You get one life and a lot of last days. Why not look through new eyes and plan a new path, which likely includes much of the old path but cleaned up, straightened, and with a higher purpose? Why not make certain that what's important, or exciting, or flat-out incredible is *yours*—by intent, not happenchance?

The alternative isn't dreadful. It's just more todays forever. It's what 99.98% of all people have done since the discovery of fire and ashtrays. And what almost all of your friends will do (unless you're kind enough to share this book with them).

But why would *you* leave something as important as 30 years of your only life to fate, chance, or fortune. Or, worse yet, your memory!

Why wouldn't you congratulate yourself for all of the good things you've done, take a long look at the what you've yet to do, dip into your dream bag to see what more you could add to the roster, factor in your health and coffers, touch base with

"Any plan that depends upon luck to succeed isn't a plan; it's a gamble."

The last days of your only life

"Old age isn't bad when you consider the alternative."

Maurice Chevalier

your mate, then put all that down on paper, creating a clear map of where you intend to go to finish the journey that was earlier interrupted (by sex, confusion, frustration, mayhem, at least one incredibly daft boss, and bad music) but is now open to completion?

Before we delve into planning, let's address two related concerns, in reverse order of importance. The first asks, "If this planning a Super Second Life is such a hot idea, why didn't my folks do it?" Of all the dumb stuff they did do, they never mentioned it.

The second is more important. It simply says that it doesn't matter what we plan, we're going to lose or forget about the plans, give up on them, or just laugh at the exercise a few months after it's finished. Heavens. More on that in a moment.

So, why weren't our folks as wise as we are when it comes to creating a specific plan for the second half of our lives? Four reasons come quickly to mind:

1. Their expectations came directly from what they'd seen their parents do. In our grandparents' time, few lived beyond 60 and they were patterned into a life of working until retirement, then hanging on until death.
2. Our grandparents probably lived at home (or within a mile) and in effect were dependents again, so there was no reason to plan. They usually had chores to perform and were a vital part of the household.
3. Even if they wanted to work longer or lead more active lives, the number of available service jobs were extremely limited, travel was much harder, and as long as they lived at or near home and spent within their pension or Social Security allotments, there was little incentive to do more.
4. And they were just plumb tired. Labor then meant manual, at work or at home, and jobs demanded plenty of it. The key part of "retirement" was "tire." Add a "d" and any stimulus to a vital, active post-work life was gone. Medicines and treatment were still relatively primitive, nutrition was substandard, and one's stamina at 55 was like a 75 year-old's today.

We're on our own!

"The first forty years of life give us the text; the next thirty supply the commentary on it."

Arthur Schopenhauer

Today, our lives now are markedly different. At 55, we still have those extra 30 years to live. Even if our kids did expect us to return home, there's no room. Instead, they more likely expect us to be independent as long as we can, then slip into some sort of aided-living home before we die in a hospital. They would be grateful if we did this without interrupting their schedules; doubly grateful if we simply told them what we had done after the fact. Except death. If we die without prewarning them, they'll never forgive us. A few day's warning is perfect.

They presume we will patch together the government support—Social Security and Medicare—and add our pension, insurance, and savings to it to have enough money to take care of all future needs, including medical and burial. If we don't do this, we are irresponsible. (They wouldn't refuse a small inheritance either.)

Not that we'll be completely detached. The telephone can keep us in touch if we have emergency needs. And we aren't nearly as isolated as our grandparents were, with radio (we still listen to radios), television, computers, and sometimes accessible public transport (after driving becomes difficult).

As long as we don't mortify our kids (tiptoeing, out of sight, is best), we can even do "young" things and no one seems to care.

In fact, we're not as old as our counterparts decades back. We eat better, do less physically taxing work, keep working longer, pay more attention to our health, have more information at our disposal about maintaining a healthy life, exercise, have more seniors to mix with, are far more open about mental health, and have a stronger web of services we can draw upon.

So why shouldn't we plan our own best lives for the second half? Society is indifferent (though it will try to sell us anything it thinks we're addled enough to buy). Our kids are permissive; turnabout is indeed fair play. It's our money, what there is of it, and our time, which is more abundant. And, to repeat, "here we are, feeling fine, looking good, full of ginger, all bucketed up and historically with no place to go." May as well mortify the kids and do what we want when we want. The meter's ticking. If we plan it right, we can be a constant 30-year mortification machine.

We've still got plenty of marbles!

"The years between fifty and seventy are the hardest. You are always asked to do things, and yet you are not decrepit enough to turn them down."

T.S. Eliot

Learning

The supposition that whether we plan a "Super Second Life" or not, we'll be incapable of carrying out the plans or will lose interest sounds suspiciously like saying that we begin the mental and attitudinal slippery slide sometime in the 50s (or sooner), and it gets progressively faster and steeper until we're lucky to find our shoes, much less tie them, when we reach antiquity. (Go Velcro!)

Sometimes that is true, and then it's not at all funny. There are mental disorders, but they hold steady at about 5% of the populace at every age. Seniors have no edge there. And there are forms of latter-life dementia and illnesses, including of course Alzheimer's. They are tragedies for all involved.

But most folks don't change much during their later years, beyond the usual physical aging and decline in short-term memory. The fear of mental incompetence is for most groundless. The danger is that we will accept the false assumption that all mental functions decline with age, then act out the stereotype, withdrawing and losing self-esteem and becoming a self-fulfilling prophecy.

Intelligence tests show little change as one ages, although one gets slower (and more cautious). We do process sensory information slower and take longer to perceive a stimulus, and slower yet when the task is complicated or a surprise. "We continue to gain rather than decline in our ability to manage our daily affairs; it is usually only in times of stress or loss that our mechanisms may be pushed beyond their limits," says Dr. Mark E. Williams in *The Complete Guide to Aging and Health*.

Even better, our response to physical stimulus needn't change at all—and will actually be faster if we take part in regular physical activity.

Three second life components deserve comment: learning, satisfaction with life, and personal control.

Our capacity to learn continues throughout life. That capacity is divided into three phases of information processing: encoding, storage, and retrieval.

Encoding is mentally registering information. We get worse at it as we age, but that may be linked to hearing or vision—barriers to having the information understood. We are best when we can link visual information to its audio component.

Our recall ability, to search and retrieve information from storage, worsens over time, but there is little decline in our ability to match our information in storage with information in the environment.

While our short-term memory is the biggest change with aging (what did I say?), our long-term memory declines only a bit, and that is probably due to poorer encoding. Very long-term memory gets better from 20-50 and holds steady until about 70. Maybe it is overwhelmed after 70 because we've gathered up so much to remember!

Mostly we compensate and get along fine (as long as we pin our keys to our sleeve and write where we're going on our hand). What throws us off is a new challenge, like new surroundings, or major stress, like the loss of a spouse.

Satisfaction and control

One imagines that the older we get, the less satisfied with life we become. Except for the extremely old, life satisfaction doesn't decrease with age, despite all the factors that could influence it, like poorer health, loss of a spouse or friends, and less money or activity. People simply adapt to those situations that can't be changed. And elders report less stress: they cope better and expect less.

A lot of it has to do with attitude. "The attitude we take about aging will be very important in affecting the success with which we age," says Dr. Williams. "Meaningful participation in family and community activities is a major source of personal satisfaction and is the product of cultural attitudes and decisions made earlier in life."

A plan for a purposeful second life could play a key role in that later level of personal satisfaction.

A sense of personal control is critical to our overall well-being. Personal control is the ability to manipulate aspects of our environment, and the inability to do that results in feelings of helplessness and depression. A loss of perceived control can happen to older folk, particularly when they have a disability. It can produce adverse affects (rage, depression, violence, abuse), even death. They simply give up.

Which is, again, where a plan for life built of choices is useful. Even if all of the plans fail to materialize, just the ability to predict events may be a form of control in that it allows us to adapt to the situation.

Dr. Williams adds,

> The acceptance of limits and a finite future is a quality of maturity, not a matter of resignation or defeat. With years of rich experience and reflection, some of us can transcend our own circumstances. We call this ability to see the truth in the light of the moment, wisdom. So as we age in creativity, in deepening wisdom and sensibility we become *more*, not less. And we realize that aging confronts us with the tension between ourselves now and ourselves in the future. We have an enormous amount of choice regarding our own aging. What are we sowing, and what is it we wish to reap?"

More about our physical and mental health in Chapter 6.

Planning and choice, then, is what this book is about. Plan and choose how you will best use this 30-year gift; how you will keep your body and mind tuned and in control of a life loved and fully lived.

"Age is a bad habit which a busy man has no time to form."

Emile Herzog

What Base Did You Build During Those First 40+ Years?

2

We're all nature's slaves until we're useless to the breeding imperative, and most of what we did—particularly from about 12 through the 20s (and even 30s)—was basically out of our control.

Nonetheless, you got taught, learned skills, found values, developed a personality, and discovered areas of strength and passion that you want to be part of your life forever.

Whatever the cause, you came to love tennis, teaching, baking, or painting on wood. A future life without work, reading, golf, playing with the grandtykes, or doodling in web graphics would be unthinkable.

And you gathered up achievements in specific disciplines or directions while you grew up. Along the way you found things you wanted to explore in depth or experience first-hand when you no longer needed the job income, when time was your own.

So here you start recording those strengths, passions, and directions that you want to carry over into your Super Second Life, to become a part, even the core, of your later life Action Plan. And what you want to leave properly behind.

You identify the things you particularly value today to include in your coming Super Second Life.

---

*We are busy,
walking wonders*

If we ever began with a *tabula rasa*—that famous blank slate upon which our history is written—it is brim full by the time we're 40 or 50, with squiggly notes on the sides and a couple of Post-Its wagging off the edge.

We've managed to cram in more living in the first half of our lives than we imagine or give ourselves credit for.

The bigger achievements we acknowledge, and detail on our résumés and curriculum vitae: schools attended, degrees or certificates attained, jobs or positions held, and awards received.

And we're certain to recall the people we married, children brought into the world, places lived, and hobbies or special events enjoyed.

But there's a lot of other things we take for granted that would seem extraordinary if seen from peasant's eyes centuries back. They have given us a depth unimagined by even the most visionary not that long ago.

*Think of all
we have done...*

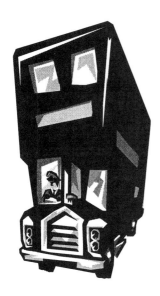

We have probably visited a half-dozen foreign countries, yet even if we've never left our state, through television, movies, and videos we can draw real sweat from vicariously paddling through a steamy forest in New Guinea or gasping for oxygen climbing those last 200 yards up the snowy, swirling Mount Everest.

Without even knowing how it's done, we can e-mail to Bali, find an exotic recipe for *feijoada baiana*, or bid on a newly found Grecian vase.

We drive cars more powerful and dangerous than a herd of buffalo, read whole books, write whole letters, hear music performed by symphony orchestras half a globe away, understand depression, successfully interact with more people in one day than our ancestors saw in a lifetime, and live whole lives without need of a weapon.

We are, flat-out, walking wonders, with a brain that would be the marvel of any world. In our own, we are top dogs: animals know things, but we know that we know things. We balance jobs, families, necessities, fun, and charity, with time left over to flirt, read to our kids, whistle, daydream, and shingle a shed.

What's next?

Some defining tools should help

So what we've done in our first 40 or 50 years would astound our grandparents and be utterly unbelievable to their grandparents.

Whew! That was just the first half. We've still got 30 years left—a whole second life, into which we bring knowledge, polished skills, friends, professional contacts, maturity, social stability, enough street savvy to at least not lose what we possess, enough humor to stay sane and do our business, and enough vigor and cunning to pick out which cards we need to play a winning hand.

After all, our first life doesn't just end and all that we gathered disappear.

In fact, we must create an awareness of having two lives, which is a secondary purpose of this book. We must, at some point, realize that much of what worked in our early years was needed then but is inappropriate, if not counterproductive, later. At the gateway between those lives we must become the gatekeeper, to take stock and let pass most of the skills and knowledge, stop many of the behaviors and attitudes that were nature-driven but are useless after fertility becomes impossible or irrelevant, and question much of the rest. More on those behaviors in Chapter 4.

The problem is determining what we want to let into our second lives.

The second half of this book will indeed help us define what we want to do during those latter years, and, by extension, what is needed to make that happen.

If we've been hapless scoundrels the first half, there's much to be left behind plus a new attitude and supportive skills to obtain for life number two. If we led a driven, job-intensive life but now want to pursue a second career interspersed with much travel and filmmaking, we're on the path to making that happen.

Of course, we will continue to learn, adding new knowledge and skills to our slate in the second half. If it's necessary later, we will acquire what we don't have now, just as we did in our first life.

*Looking backward
to see forward*

At this point, a few tools might help us tend that gate. They will also be helpful later when we design our "Super Second Life."

The most important is a no-nonsense look at what we did in our first life. More than another résumé, it is our own listing of what was important, what we learned from it, what we want to discontinue now, what we want to take with us into our second life, and, after looking at all that, what comes to mind that would add joy and worth to our coming years.

It's your turn! Let's do this by creating five "me now" lists that will help you see more clearly who you are now and who you would like to be in your second life. The lists overlap because some related questions are asked different ways. There is something to be learned from each list, so you'd be best served by doing all five.

But if you don't do any, okay. Or just two or three. Nor is there a grade for excellence, incisiveness, or honesty. The lists can simply help add definition and richness to those coming 30 years.

The first list, appropriately List 1, is the most complex. It asks you to catalogue the most important contributions you have made in your first 40 (or whatever) years, in order of importance. After the contributions, continue to list your achievements, then the activities you performed, also in the order of the satisfaction or pride they brought you. Then, from each item noted, identify the skills developed or strengthened from that contribution, achievement, or activity. Finally, ways you might apply that skill in your second life.

Expand the length of the lists as needed. Remember, the same lists, usually longer, are found in the Appendix. *Also, if you are using a library book or one for public use, please copy the examples in the Appendix and write on those!*

"There's hardly a man alive who could not retire very comfortably in his old age if he could sell his experience for what it cost him."

"ME NOW" LIST 1		
Contributions Achievements Activities	Skills Developed	Ways I might apply these skills in my second life...

List 1 speaks of skills. List 2 describes you as a person: as you are now and have been, adjectives one might have used to describe you earlier but are no longer applicable, and new adjectives you'd like them to use during your second life.

Why are you doing this? To stop and take stock now, to set up a temporary mental comparison between the way you are now (and were), and to begin to set up some vision (and goals) of how you wish to be (and what you may wish to do) in the future.

"ME NOW" LIST 2		
An objective person would use these adjectives to describe me now	Adjectives no longer applicable that they might have used about me in my first life	New adjectives I would like them to properly use about me during my second life

The third list asks a similar question but from a broader perspective. First, ten words that would describe your first life. Then, of those ten, which words would you like to continue to describe your second life?

"ME NOW" LIST 3	
These 10 words describe my first life:	I'm putting an "X" by those that I want to continue to describe my second life
1.	
2.	
3.	
4.	
5.	
6.	
7.	
8.	
9.	
10.	

List 4 is broader yet, and asks for more future projections. It asks what you want to leave at the gate, what you want to carry into your second life, and what additional strengths you wish to develop in your second life.

"ME NOW" LIST 4		
These are attitudes, activities, traits, etc. that I want to leave at the gate	These are strengths I now possess that I want to take into my second life	These are strengths I want to develop in my second life

Life should be a joy, not just work and worry. The fifth list, but one column wide, doesn't require retrospection but simply asks you to list ten words that would add *joy* and *worth* to your "Super Second Life."

"ME NOW" LIST 5
These 10 words would add joy and worth to my "Super Second Life"
1.
2.
3.
4.
5.
6.
7.
8.
9.
10.

What to keep; what to leave

Did you doubt that you had a trove of skills and abilities you were honing during your first life? Look back at your lists, then reflect on how much better prepared you are now to fully live than you were before.

That's what you're bringing into your second life. And what you're leaving behind, as unneeded, undesired, or detrimental to where you want to be this time around.

We don't have a clear view yet of what these next 30 years could be like, but these exercises will help define that plan later.

For now, congratulate yourself on doing them and on caring enough about yourself to have read this far. And give yourself a "good job" on having not only survived this long, but with so much going for you. After all, you're here, intact, and eager to move on. And now you know the secret: the first half is just a loud, sweaty exercise to get you tuned up and mentally ready to live your "Super Second Life!"

How much is your Super Second Life worth?

For some, another day or month of life might be worth a fortune. For 30 years, many fortunes!

But for the rest of us, with no fortunes to spare, let's let William Shakespeare suggest a value. He let Richard III set a price when he shouted "A horse! A horse! My kingdom for a horse."

You are the king or queen of your life; it is your kingdom—with your home your castle. So if somebody offered to sell you a whole extra year of life, an entire year in which you could do what you wanted—sail or golf or work or just kick back and read more Shakespeare (or frothy romances)—would that be worth a horse a year?

What's a good horse worth? Maybe $2,000? Plus oats and necessities—another $500? Thus a year might be worth $2,500.

Yet most of us, on the average, get 30 full years. That's 30 times $2,500. Our Super Second Life, then, by this odd logic, would be a free gift of $75,000!

If somebody gave me $75,000 with no strings attached but to spend it, I'd sure make a plan before I let the green fly. Which is all this book suggests: you're going to get the gift anyway, so stop now and figure out the best way to use it as fully and with as much joy as possible. Stop horsing around.

Who Should Create Your Super Second Life?

3

Let me ask the question again. "Who should create your Super Second Life?"

You.

Not your spouse, your parent(s), your kid(s), the government, your job, or society.

If you've got a mate or dependents, make your own Action Plan, then integrate them into it using the conflict resolution process explained in Chapter 15.

But single, joined, or encumbered, it's your time.

These are the only last years you will ever have. Why waste them? And why try to live somebody else's life at the expense of your own? It's not only impossible, it's a huge waste of your happiness and your potential.

So, you do your own planning. NOW.

Single, mated, or encumbered, you do your planning. It's your life.

It's your life

You must create your own Super Second Life. Who else? It's *your* life.

The days and what you do with them belong to you—not to your spouse, your parent(s), your kid(s), society, or anyone else.

21

They are the only days you will ever have. At any age, sitting around waiting for life to lead you somewhere is still just sitting around. You need a plan for what you will do for the rest of your life: *your own plan*.

You're married or have dependents or others you are responsible for? Join the club! Let's address that a bit later in this chapter.

You are important

The point of these pages is personal responsibility. *You* are important. *You* bring things to this life that no one else can. *You* have a life that counts. *You*.

You can decide to simply live out your days, unplanned, letting circumstances and others direct your fate. (In which case you should stop reading this book; it will frustrate you.)

Or you can be proactive and mold those days as much as you wish or can. You can determine what's important to you and to those you love. You can select what you'd like to learn more about, or see, or experience. You can decide who gets your primary attention, who you want to help, what causes are sufficiently important to deserve your support and promotion, where you want to live, how you can make your life part of a better city, group, or universe—whatever you want!

You can reshape your next 30 years

Is that selfish? Too self-centered? Hardly. If *you* don't take responsibility for yourself and how you will spend your days, then somebody else may have to—and that *is* selfish. They have their own lives to tend to and live.

One alternative, of course, is to take care of others' lives rather than or in addition to your own. Which won't work. You can help others in times of need, but you can no more control their lives than you can direct the wind or manage the stars. And why would you, assuming that your own responsibility is a full-time job?

The ideal is for loving people, all assuming responsibility for their own lives, to then share the extra love that overflows.

What does that mean as it relates to your own Super Second Life? It means that you not only think about what you want to do with your extra 30 years, you convert those thoughts into words. Since there is more to doing than simply wishing, it also means that all the variables become part of that plan, including your time, finances, energy, and state of health.

Most of us didn't plan our first life, but we can do better in the second

Most of us did little or no true planning up to this point. Oh sure, we made spot decisions when required, and planned for short trips and how to invest or which car to buy, but full, detailed life plans are about as rare in those under 40 as teeth in worms. Perhaps rightly so: we are under others' control the first half of that time. We live in a trance.

It's curious how we finally get control just about the time that men and women start heading in different directions. For every man who suddenly finds feelings and realizes that winning every race is very, very tiring (if not impossible) there is a woman who suddenly starts itching to get going, in a new-found voice that blows the more timid aside.

If people are going to wake up from their trance and take full reins, it is usually when they are from about 35 to 55, although some do it earlier. That is when we can cut out what isn't working from our youth, build on what is, and focus on solidifying our working and home lives.

This book proposes that we also project from that point until our last days. That each person take responsibility for their entire lives, to maximize the skills and knowledge gathered to create the very best Super Second Life possible.

Mates and dependents are people too!

Oh yes, those mates and dependents.

Guess what—they have lives too, however much you suspect they'd like you to plan and lead theirs for them.

So what I'm proposing is no less valid for them to do than it is for you.

There may be exceptions, for you or them. If you are terminally ill and have but a few months left, make a quicker plan, then get living fully now and each remaining day. (Studies show that people who do this are not only happier, they tend to live longer and some heal from their illnesses.)

"We are all, it seems, saving ourselves for the Senior Prom. But many of us forget that somewhere along the way we must learn to dance."

Alan Harrington

But most of us have no such guarantee. We're going to sludge along until our clocks stop (in seconds or 30 years or longer), so we have no excuse. What is tricky is working out the interrelated details with dependents.

For mates, both you and they should create a personal Action Plan. The financial resources will clearly overlap. Then get together and see how the plans can be made compatible and mutually supportive. A great tool for actual or potential conflict resolution is explained in Chapter 15 that can soften the edges and help synchronize goals for the exciting years ahead.

Dependents need their own Action Plan too, 40-plus or at any age.

Your children will, hopefully, be on their own by the time you hit 55, but if that is not the case then that special relationship must be factored into your Action Plan. Start by creating your own dream list as if that were not an issue. Then modify your plans to make both your assistance to your children still in need of you and your own grander plan are mutually realizable.

Whether you are single, joined, or otherwise encumbered, it's still *your* life and *your* time.

You do your own planning. Now.

What is Inappropriate to Repeat the Second Time Around—and What is Essential?

If nature hadn't been in control those first 40 years, we'd all be as extinct as the puffed oozoo.

She had rules and a tight rein, but you outlasted her. You escaped—full of zest! You're free!

You can toss out the foolishness of the teens, forget the steam of "romantic love," quit leaping into bed just to prove you can, stop hunting for unconditional acceptance in all the wrong places, discontinue supporting your kids, and get rid of half your four-sizes-too-small wardrobe. Oh yes, the beauty contest has also ended—who cares?

Baggy boppers or sagging surfers don't cut it. It's time for something far more important than your species—you!

So what you need to know in this chapter is what is different in the post-40 years than before. What does freedom from nature really mean? What do we want to keep in our Super Second Lives? And what of the past is now simply an embarrassing waste of time and energy to repeat— and progressively less fitting as we truly mature.

Stop! Am I suggesting a Super Second Life without love, sex, or even rock-'n-roll? Why go on? Pass the vial. What could possibly replace them?

Real love, real sex, and maybe real music.

It's time to complete two guide lists, "In" and "Out," so we can pack appropriately for the liberating journey in the decades to come...

Shows why we acted like we did—and what we can toss overboard the second time around.

Too old for foolishness

The hardest period for most of us is from 40-55, when a mindset honed in our earlier years to create adulation from peers and gratification any old way is suddenly the wrong notes to the wrong tune. We've outgrown the foolishness. We're dancing fools one day, regular fools the next.

What won hearts and accolades suddenly looks foolish. Where heads spun our direction, we've become instantly invisible. We were strutting down our road leading the pack. Now nothing looks familiar, and the only map we have points backwards.

Odder yet, as bewildered as we are, we don't really care all that much. If we could afford to be honest, or find anybody else who really cared or could understand, we'd admit that we're getting tired of the "youth game." The primping and posturing and the hustle suddenly aren't worth their salt.

Barbara Sher says it better

Nobody captures better the pain and retrospective humor of those first 40 years than Barbara Sher in ***It's Only Too Late if You Don't Start Now***. She lived through them. She survived the hormonal mist. And now she provides a liberating map to freedom.

Let me summarize her retrospective look at us in nature's servitude.

Barbara says that the first 40 years aren't ours. That's when we pay our dues to nature. Our turn comes only when we get too old to breed. Having babies, being the fairest of the lot, and protecting our kids like crazy (until they give that craziness back to us) are the driving forces of youth. The bus stops are Beauty, Rebellion, Making It, and Doing It—is it any wonder we're frazzled by now? But a great transformation happens in the 40s when nature kicks us out.

Until then we are slaves to cultural narcissism. If you doubt it, look at when we were babies. When we were hungry, we screamed for food. When we were ignored or didn't get our way? More screaming. Our parents obeyed another mandate: they fed and loved us like we were the universe itself. Both were vital to keeping our species alive.

We relentlessly tried to hold on to that most-favored status that was the core of our first life. We learned that parents pulled back, others scowled, and eventually we couldn't be the center of everybody's existence, let alone that universe. But we never really gave up—until we had no choice. The game just changed. When puberty descended, we switched love fonts to the other sex. Nobody is to blame. It was a domino effect that ensured we would leave our childhood homes to find mates, reproduce as often as possible, and protect our children until they were old enough to do the same.

There is a biological purpose to this. The drama of this loss of unconditional love and our relentless struggle to get it back again is designed to save our species. That's why we compete obsessively with our siblings for attention. That's why we walk out on our unfair families at adolescence, in search of someone who will love us as we should be loved. That's why we try to be beautiful and successful and worthy of being adored again. That's also why we respond to the love our own infants feel for us—and only us—by falling madly in love with them.

And that's why we're thrown into panic at midlife, because we suddenly realize we're going to lose the battle. That we are mortal. The struggle to maintain some version of center stage is not only exhausting, we will lose.

The first 40 years belong to biology, not to us. And as we age and start to sag, spread, and lose hair, in comparison to others half our age, we're supposed to feel unhappy and try harder—we might just produce another baby!

Yet mankind has made huge technological advances. We simply stay younger and live longer than ever before—long after we are of any value to the species.

Something very curious happens during those years of enslavement. There are brief moments when we escape, when nature doesn't need us as badly. Three intermissions. The first is from the age of about 8 to 11, when we can take care of ourselves and become exceptional creatures, our most clear and creative selves, interested in friends, eager to learn. Then the hormones switch! The second intermission is somewhere in our twenties or early 30s, when we've found a satisfying love relationship, are married, and plan for or have babies. The third is after 40.

What do we have to look forward to in the third, open-ended intermission? Less beauty, less power, less status, less health, less love, less sex. (Or so nature thinks.) Then death.

Sounds awful.

But in fact it's a true blessing, a transformative time like no other that humans in the past have known. Another 30 or 40 years of freedom, unbound by nature, to be the best person we can.

And where might we look for insight into how the second life might be? To the 8-11 year-old, says Sher. An imp who wasn't afraid of either sex, who ran and cycled and let their body and mind roam. Who was funny, inquisitive, spirited. Who hadn't much use for money (since they seldom had any) and even less patience for pains and sickness.

Now it's time to capture the essence of that winged sprite, to find that creative center and to build from it. To find that amazing clarity and sense of self, an unconflicted ability to love learning, to experience unpossessive affection for friends... To let go of the craziness of the teen years and the head-down doggedness of the working years and regain control of the last years, to take into them the best of all the things we learned, to plan, then fulfill a Super Second Life from the moorings of the past.

How does this pertain to me and my Super Second Life?

We're crossing the Rubicon that separates our youth from our mature second life. We alone carry our future baggage, on tired shoulders and aching knees. We cross but once, so things must be left behind.

Here we make choices or *we* are left behind, a graying, anxious impostor who refuses to make the tribal cleansing required to become an elder.

One of the most difficult tasks of designing a truly personal Super Second Life is deciding what must be abandoned and which of the core values and dreams are consistent with post-breeding, full-adult maturity. Those we want to carry and nurture.

In Chapter Two we got a first glimpse of what we did in those first 40 years that we'd like to expunge now and in the future. On the Me Now Lists we wrote those adjectives and definitions that others (and we) might use to describe our first life. We noted the words identified with the earlier us that we don't want to perpetuate, and we described the attitudes, activities, and traits we want to leave on this side of the Super Second Life gate. (Many of those overlapped because, looking into the same well from different angles, we sometimes saw the same things.)

Later in this chapter we will focus even tighter on those things that can enhance our full enjoyment of the liberation that nature has unwittingly granted us—for living so long. We will create two personal guide lists to help us steer the course. What better titles than "In" and "Out"?

Now, let's take a no-nonsense, objective look at our first 40 (or 45, 50 or 55) years to determine which behaviors and thought patterns we want to keep and those that have run their course and no longer serve our present or future needs. We might also find behaviors that never were beneficial (and deserve to be excised immediately), plus others so excessive that they must be questioned hard and let into our future only with clear restrictions and on a tight leash, if at all. (Drugs, booze, false pride, an outsized ego, overpowering sexuality, and perhaps smoking come immediately to mind.)

We will then list the behaviors that no longer work alongside those accomplishments, strengths, and positive personal traits we now possess and want to maintain, plus new strengths and traits we wish to create and develop in the years to come, to form the action outline of our Super Second Life.

Future accomplishments are less important. They will more likely come from life activities rather than from setting and achieving hard-and-fast goals. A Super Second Life for most will probably be less about seeking laurels and fattening dossiers than enjoyably being all that we can be (in mufti)—while having fun in the doing and growing. Less a future of "notches" than heart-felt feelings and smiles of satisfaction.

"Old age is when our vices quit us."

La Rochefoucauld

But we must be kind to ourselves when we look back at the moon surface of our past. We must delight in the peaks but not dwell unduly long on the depths and prairies. Some of the less delightful sites had very little to do with us. From what we did wrong or could have been done better—the dumb choices, those secret caves of cowardice, the missed opportunities—we must learn the lessons they teach, then forget them. Nobody gets through the first 40 or 50 years unbruised. We must clean the slate as best we can. We get a second chance in a Super Second Life.

Loss?

What will we lose in our Super Second Life? Beauty and good looks, power and status, health, and love and sex. Then we get death.

Let's discuss each of them here, to see what baggage we can gratefully leave or discard on our journey into a new empire, where we are the emperor or empress.

Beauty and Good Looks

Nobody looks younger by growing older, except at the odd moments in our mind and heart. So what's the big deal? We'll have to surrender eventually. The only question is how.

We can respond in four ways to the bulging beltline or sagging skin.

We can resist with all our might. Become gym junkies; jump to Jazzercise. Tummy tucks. Face lifts. Chest hair implants. Liposuction. What we can't do is buy youth. We can just etch the illusion, then count the days.

We can yield slowly and strike a compromise with nature. Do what we can to preserve the activity and spunk of youth but respect time's calling. Stay in shape, eat healthful foods in modest quantities, switch to diet soda and low-cal dressing, protect ourselves from the sun, and keep a humor prod in hand to slow down nature's advances.

> "Middle age is when your age starts to show around your middle."
>
> *Bob Hope*

We can stop playing the game altogether, blend in, keep clean, and look elsewhere for more important values. Accept that aging is part of our heritage, take particular care of our minds and souls, keep our bodies fit and strong, and find new challenges to fill our days and nights.

Or we can go hog wild and not only yield to nature, become part of it. We can flee the normal conventions, toss our shoes, throw on a loin cloth, and slide back to the wild. The question is why.

"Easy for you to say!" you say, but who will love us when we look like our mother or father? Maybe ourselves, finally.

Beauty and good looks seem so superficial to be concerned about, but they aren't. In the U.S. we will spend four billion dollars a year on our appearance by 2002. Part of us knows that we could better spend that money, time, and energy elsewhere. But a second part feels like another power is pulling our beauty strings—try as we may, they are completely out of our hands. Too many strands of the past, too much media and conditioning, are wrapped in how we look (or how we think others think we look) for us to quickly set them straight. The pretty people won the crowns and we were left to do the best we could with plain, damaged, or at best mediocre goods.

We learned to get by. We even got degrees, ran companies, wrote best sellers, and painted our way into museums while, we imagined, the pretty people married each other and posed. We did our best with what we had. But now even that is seeping away. There's only one consolation: we'll all be ugly in the end!

The saddest part is that all of it is such a waste. The only advantage nature wanted from the extra plumage and surface beauty was that we'd sire or have babies, and almost everybody had them anyway.

In our second life, new babies are rock bottom on anybody's list of priorities, at least new babies of our own. We're not as particular about siring.

So logic would suggest that the other skills and learning and values we gathered during our first life will be far more important the second time around, and that beauty and good looks will be reduced to health, vigor, cleanliness, and comfort.

That leaves us with the question, What do we leave behind as we begin our second life journey? Old thinking about the role of our appearance. Dressing to try to resurrect that "old you," or a you that you wish had existed. Clothes and body decoration that is blatantly inappropriate for who we are. Body deformation in the name of beauty.

What new attitudes do we embrace for the coming years? That we dress precisely how we feel and wish. If a boa, party dress, and slippers (or a T-shirt and a Zoot suit) make sense and would feel best, that's it—even to go shopping or renew a driver's license. That comfort is important, and what that means can change as our bodies change. That it's nobody's business but ours how we look and dress. But that we also won't use dress and appearance to intentionally embarrass ourselves or others, and if we do, we will find out what that is telling us and make needed modifications. Finally, that cleanliness is the minimum guide, for our own health, sense of well-being, and worth, as well as the comfort and concern of others.

Power and status

At some point in our Super Second Lives we will surely lose the power and status we now enjoy. But we will almost as surely acquire a new kind of serenity, which is a softer kind of personal power. And we might find new status too, if we want it.

Age doesn't necessarily diminish one's effectiveness or control. Popes have remained in power beyond their hundredth birthday, many acting heads of state ruled in their 80s, U.S. Presidents held office in their 70s, and the corporate world is dotted with chiefs 65+. Not to mention artists, writers, sculptors, architects, and others plying singular skills who performed at their peak far past their life expectancy. In some tribes you must be old before you can tell tribal stories. Only professional sports find active participants bowing out by 40 or thereabouts, knuckleball pitchers and Satchel Paige excepted.

In fact, in today's hectic world those at the top seldom get the luxury of thinking about relinquishing their power until they hit six score. In their 40s or 50s, while they may be easing into a new life phase in terms of beauty or love, they'll still need a full bag of business skills, plus the vigor to exercise them. Releasing power, or being released from it, for most comes with voluntary or forced retirement. Status can linger longer.

Perhaps the hardest part of having power and status is knowing when and how to give them up—or to stop trying to retain them. Thus an important new element to add to our skill bag from about 40-50 on is an "exit plan." A set of steps that will let us continue to practice what we do best and enjoy most in a new arena, outside the direct employment realm or in a new job or firm.

We can also carry over the skills that create power and status into second life activities, like fund-raising and voluntary philanthropic or community-enhancing positions.

A related concern finds those with power and status so involved in reaching that position that they never develop extra-employment interests, hobbies, or even concerns. So when they find themselves unemployed and outside their comfort zone, they are lost. They have no place to reinvest their talents and energy. To offset this, then, another element to develop from 40 on are fields of interest where we can quickly shift when our last check is received and before the gold watch stops ticking.

There's more to say about power. Most of us aren't CEOs or moguls. We are everyday people somewhere in the cogs of business or are homemakers or run small companies or act on a stage. If we have mogul power, or much power at all, somebody forgot to tell us. Status? Only to the new hire or a new wife to whom anybody with more experience has status. That's unimportant. We still have the same kinds of stress, too many things to do in too little time, and pressure to achieve. We just want a break sometime somewhere to live and do what's important to us, or what should be important if we just had enough time to figure it out. And we suspect the moguls want the same thing.

We're hoping that the treadmill will at least slow down after we've learned the job, the kids are on their own, and our Super Second Life drops in.

Why wait that long? What we all share, hustling honchos and weary workers, is our obsession with control. As if we can somehow regulate the universe's throttle or alter the grander flow of life by our daily activities.

What we can do is affect our immediate universes in small ways. We can stand up for what's right. We can take action against greed and selfishness. But we're not omniscient, and we cannot do more than our best thoughts and actions which, if used as our guides, would bring us more personal acceptance and pride. It would inject far more reality and balance into our stressed worlds.

So what we might add to our skills-to-learn and perfect later would be a decided attempt to bring order and serenity to our present chaos. To do our best at all times, focus on the essentials, and learn to let the forces of life that do control kick in and do their part. Unless we are gods, that is our limit.

Then, when whatever power or status we have in others' eyes diminishes and our ego is disengaged, two true elements of lifelong happiness, clarity and serenity, will be in place to govern during our Super Second Life. And we will have had the benefit of honing and enjoying them in the meantime.

What don't we want to carry over the bridge? Obsession with control, chaos, self-inflicted stress, false gods, others' values, dishonest loyalty, irrational guilt, and any tendrils of shame.

Health

Health is so important that Chapter 6 is dedicated to it. The quality and length of our Super Second Life will be a direct result of our genetic inheritance, how we cared for ourselves in our first life, and what we do to maintain a healthy regimen in our coming days.

By health we mean the whole package, body and mind. So we will look in depth what aging does to both, what we can modify at the gate, and where we should focus after 40.

For now, what, in summary, do we want "in" our second life? Everything sensible that will foster better health and a better, longer life.

Out? The reverse, particularly anything that we are doing in our 40s and 50s (and earlier) that will compromise our health and positive longevity.

Love and Sex

You thought we'd never get to the love and sex!

Actually, there's two kinds of love—let's call them "romantic love" and "true love"—and I suppose a thousand kinds of sex, but the generic (sometimes steamy) kind will do.

Romantic love is nature-driven, baby-producing, fleeting, usually heart-breaking, and certainly misnamed. Think teenagers and early twenties, though it lingers until the 40s or longer. Read passion, lust, "in love," hot sex, and maybe addiction.

True love usually comes later, can last forever, involves friendship, can also yield babies, and is even embraced by theologians. Sex too, as part of true love—sometimes hot but almost always more playful.

Let's use a left hand-right hand analogy.

The left hand stands for romantic love. This hand moves in one direction only, toward us, when we want to be loved. It grabs a mate and pulls them in. The criteria are few: a person who provides flesh for our private movies or dreams—what they lack in virtues or brilliance we will mentally provide. Barbara Sher says it best, "Romantic love (is) nothing but hunger, hormones, and illusion."

That it has a "mind of its own" is giving the left hand too much credit. There are no brain fibers there. It's granular, impetuous, relentless. And the results are wildly exciting and unforgettable, immortalized in song lyrics about impossibilities and unrequited yearning. It had better work. The propagation of our species depends on it.

When the left hand of "romantic love" starts wrinkling, shakes a bit, and becomes the topic of thinly-veiled bemusement by those a decade or two (or three) younger, every honest, red-blooded mortal knows what that hand has waiting for it: rejection, loneliness, a cold bed, and a drab, long life devoid of sparks and madness.

What foolishness. But we have to survive romantic love, infatuation, and fantasies gone wild to get to true love. Nature stuck it plunk in the way, plugged it in, and jumped aside.

Fortunately, it's on a timer, and at some point in our 40s the frenzy starts losing juice. We also get smarter the longer we

live. We realize that one-way love (me, me, me) has a built-in flaw. Our lover wants me-me-me too. Since the left hand only takes, when romantic lovers don't get our undivided and continual love, they look elsewhere. The grabbing cycle starts over. It's exhausting, disappointing, and ultimately embarrassing as the hand gets slow and desperate. At some point we're too old for such foolishness. One-night stands and hit-and-score mates require too much energy, self-deception, money, and time.

Romantic love is the opposite of true love but sometimes a conversion takes place when the sex cloud lifts and we get to truly see and like the unique person we grabbed in passion and mated in haste.

The right hand represents true love. But it needs the left because it never works alone. Together, they reach out. They embrace their mate, and the world, because true love is more than sex, it's looking at others and life with our eyes and heart wide open. It's more than a fleeting orgiastic rush, it's a running high with another person or all people, with nature, with living, and with all of life.

But it can only happen when we slow down and know who we are. It requires the stability that maturity and having identified ourselves brings. When we come to realize our own worth, our singular value, can we then see the worth and value of other people and things. We love them simply for what they are, not as we want them to be. By comparison, the high drama and electric pizzazz of romantic love shows its true colors: neon bizarre. Unplug it and there's nothing there but the echo of sizzle.

In true love we will only stay with people we like. And if we like ourselves and what we see around us, we will no longer feel that hollow, aching loneliness that romantic love always brought when the fire died. We will reach out to life to find companionship, selecting those we want near us. We will become a self-sustaining core of a radiant universe, and will want those by us to experience their own radiance as much as share ours. We will have enough love stored up to select friends. We won't need fantasies to fill in the human gaps.

"Love and memory last and will so endure until the game is called because of darkness."

Gene Fowler

There is something magnetic about people who know what they want, can choose, say no kindly but firmly, and who exude joy, curiosity, and goodness. That's who we can be when we switch from romantic to true love.

If true love sounds as bland as pale pasta, what it lacks in flash it makes up in stability and permanence, which are the strongest building blocks of a contented second life.

Fortunately, sex can remain as integral a factor as it was for romantic love, but seldom its white-hot core and often only element. It's sex at a different pace. Nothing to prove, no performance expectations. Sex to be enjoyed. Playful. Love-laden.

The myth is that with age goes the sexual desire. Humbug, says James Firman, president of the National Council on Aging in discussing a 1998 study on the topic. "For many older Americans, sex remains an important and vital part of their lives."

"Ripeness is all."
Shakespeare

According to that NCOA survey, 48% of Americans 60+ engage in sexual activity at least once a month. (The percentage would have been higher had more partners been available. There are five times as many widows as widowers in those totals. Plus 13% of the men and 44% of the women had partners with a medical condition that prevented them from having sex.) Moreover, 74% of the sexually active men and 70% of the sexually active women said they are as satisfied or even more satisfied emotionally with their sex life than they were in their 40s.

So what do we leave, internally kicking and in high dander, at the gate of the Super Second Life? The mindset and exhausting demands of romantic love. The conquest tallies; hot sheets; game-playing; sweaty risk-taking with AIDs, herpes, and other consequences; lies; pierced hearts, and the flat-out danger and all the high drama and tingle that brings.

What do we take with us, or acquire when nature turns down the voltage or we learn to override it? Lovers who talk and share, close friends who are extra-libidinous, personal contentment with who we are, the ability to say no, an eagerness to enjoy the coming years on our and life's terms, plus open eyes and an even more accepting heart.

The hardest time is indeed from about 40-55, when we still have the body, more cunning, and finally the money to play the romantic game we fumbled at and scrimped through in youth. Nature holds on with a hook, shouting "one last baby while you still can!" And while we're not too anxious about the baby, the sex still burns bright—while we still can, certain that at any moment both the desire and the ability will flee and we'll suddenly be as able, interested, and sexy as a crinkled troll.

We're half right. The desire will decrease, as much from the realization that the capture is no longer worth the hunt, and that there's another life awaiting us that simply makes more sense and is better designed to our maturing bodies and minds. Those transition years are hard ones. As much as we may try to talk ourselves out of hot sex, nature may pull us back.

But eventually it happens, then real love can too. We get other valuable Super Second Life gifts too: real friends, real sex, and more truth, honesty, and reality.

Death

If you do everything suggested in this book, you will still die. (The same will happen if you don't.) That's the nature of our beast. Sorry.

But what a run we mortals get! We get to experience love, acceptance, joy, surprise, success, happiness, even patches of ecstasy. We get to know wonderful people, see the world, run, swim, fly, ski, laugh, drive, dream, write, and read.

Of course, we don't have much say about what we do or how we are treated early on, and there are times when survival takes first call, but there are also long periods during our lives when we can direct our actions and mold our immediate environment. We can always expand our minds.

We probably have more opportunity to be our fullest and best selves during our second lives, when the rages of youth abate and wisdom (or at least experience) alights.

"Getting old is no cause for hysteria. The rose bush does not scream when the petals begin to fall."

Douglas Meador

A goal of this book is to help you extract every advantage and joy from that Super Second Life, so when Death does come knocking, your slate and your heart will be full, without regrets at what is still left undone.

Ours is a spectacular but finite world. We get one dance ticket, then the music stops. Dance!

Guide Lists:
"In" and "Out"

In Chapter Two we took a first look at our lives now, what we like and don't like. We even filled in some provisional lists, to help us clarify those thoughts.

Now we want to look more seriously at what we want to discard from our present, scattered holdings and what we want to carry into our second life, or add to it when we are there.

These are basic things, core life things. Later, we will add a Dream List of specific actions or activities we want to pursue. We will also have looked at both our health and our financial status to see what means, and restrictions, we have to make those dreams a reality.

Here we are talking more about the kind of person we would like to be, the signposts we want on our trail of daily living. To help us, we have taken a quick look at beauty, power and status, health, and love and sex. (We needn't add death to either list. The reaper always gets the last laugh.)

Time to complete more lists!

On the "In" list, write down those things, actions, traits, and thoughts you want to carry to and build from during your Super Second Life.

Conversely, put on the "Out" list anything you don't want continued from your life now (or even started later).

Like all of the lists in this book, these can be modified at will, and can be as long as you wish. (You may wish to look again at your "Me Now" lists in Chapter 2 for any ideas and insights they provide.)

Some thinking helps here, so a good way to prepare the lists is to write down the obvious items first, then add more in the minutes, hours, or days that follow, as they occur to us. Copy the lists and work on them in the off hour, adding the new items to the master list later. If done by hand, recording in pencil makes sense while the wording is finalized; then pen.

"IN" LIST
What you want to include in your Super Second Life

1.	
2.	
3.	
4.	
5.	
6.	
7.	
8.	
9.	
10.	
11.	
12.	
13.	
14.	
15.	
16.	
17.	
18.	
19.	
20.	

"OUT" LIST
What you want excluded from your Super Second Life

1.	
2.	
3.	
4.	
5.	
6.	
7.	
8.	
9.	
10.	
11.	
12.	
13.	
14.	
15.	
16.	
17.	
18.	
19.	
20.	

Reading Sources

Bortz II, Walter M., M.D., **Dare to be 100: How to Live Long and Enjoy it to the Fullest.** (Fireside, 1996). In Chapter 5, the "Gameplan," is particularly interesting.

Carter, Jimmy, **The Virtues of Aging.** (Ballantine, 1998). An excellent account of the former President and wife Rosalynn's coming to grips with their second lives.

Cassell, Christine K., M.D., ed., **The Practical Guide to Aging: What Everybody Needs to Know,** (NYU Press, 1999). Complete and easy to follow.

Dowling, Colette, **Red Hot Mamas: Coming into Our Own at 50.** (Bantam, 1996). Very funny: addresses sex, money, hormones, and menopause. For mamas of any temperature.

Dychtwald, Ken, *New Wave* (1989). Good facts showing the power and numbers of those who are or will be seniors.

Ferrin, Kelly, *What's Age Got to Do With It? Secrets to Aging in Extraordinary Ways*. (Alti, 1999). Need inspiration? 101 biographies of old folks living fully.

Kaplan, Lawrence J., *Retiring Right: Planning for Successful Retirement*. (Avery, 1990).

Lesham, Eda, *It's Better to Be Over the Hill Than Under It: Thoughts on Life Over 60* (Newmarket Press, 1990) and *Oh, To Be 50 Again!* (Times Books, 1986). For women; insightful and very funny. A journalist with a magic pen.

Lindeman, Brad, *Be an Outrageous Older Man: Action Guide for Men 50 and Beyond*. (KIT, 1998). Well written.

Oxford Book of Aging. (Oxford Press, 1994). What the older think of aging. See Mark Twain's prescription for reaching 70, p. 302.

Pipher, Mary, *Another Country: Navigating the Emotional Terrain of our Elders*. (Riverhead Books, 1999). Great insights and interviews.

Pogrebin, Letty Cottin, *Getting Over Getting Older: An Intimate Journey*. (1996). Focuses on what really counts. Very well written, with much humor. Again, for women.

Ready or Not Retirement Guide, 1995, 22nd ed. (Manpower Education Institute, 1995).

Rivers, Joan, *Don't Count the Candles (Just Keep the Fire Lit)*. (HarperCollins, 1999). Funny.

Sheehy, Gail, *New Passages: Mapping Your Life Across Time* (Random House, 1995). Gail has some newer spin-offs of this book, with update data, but this is the core book for the 50+ (as she reached 50). A very good chapter about the "Flourishing Forties" too. She's a journalist with a sociological bent. Her examples are inspiring. See p. 450 for 11 books about menopause; Sheehy wrote the key book on the topic.

Sher, Barbara, *It's Only Too Late if You Don't Start Now: How to Create Your Second Life after 40* (Delacorte Press, 1998). My favorite book to get your head right with aging. Better yet, it's funny and full of useful exercises to throttle the 40-55 tremors. Sher has other good books too—and she's older than you are!

Zelinski, Ernie J., *The Joy of Not Working* (Ten Speed Press, 3rd ed., 1997).

For a list of aging-related general organizations (with address, phone, and website), please see the Appendix.

How Do You Plan for a Three-Tiered Super Second Life?

5

Your Super Second Life is really divided into three parts: the emotionally difficult 40-55 year period; the proactive, dynamic second segment, and the reactive, reflective third.

Ideally, during the first 15 years you set the table for your Super Second Life. The second period is when most, perhaps all, of that Super Second Life takes place. The third consists of those few years (or months) when you lose independence, when comfort and survival replace growth and adventure. Some never experience the third segment at all.

This chapter focuses on defining that three-tiered reality. It also proposes that the relationships, interests, and activities pursued in the first 40 or so years make the three tiers that follow more enjoyable and eventful as well.

Ideally, the three segments seamlessly segue to create a Super Second Life.

The First Tier: 40-55 Years of Age

It seems a bit askew, if not grossly unfair, to ask us to launch a "second life" plan when we are just reaching the peak of our "first life," during the high-powered years from 40-55. That's when we hit full maturity and statistically we earn our top dollar, when our kids are growing up and our responsibility buckets are overflowing, and when we have become our own person—or should.

But, as we've already seen, they are troubled years too. Nature is getting ready to pull the plug when they start, and has left us to our wiles by the time they end. We're no longer kids, but we're not creaking old either.

We're standing in the middle of the bridge between youth and age, having seen mortality—our own—on the horizon, a horizon that doesn't look all that far away.

The Middle Years

Not surprisingly, I call these the "middle years." Not only do they fall chronologically near our mortal 50-yard line, they are also the time when our vigor, health, and performance are prime. When we have conquered the ignorance and innocence of youth but are still unfettered by the debilitation of age.

It's then we can most influence the kind of Super Second Life we might have during our later years.

Most of the money we will save for the future will be set aside, to compound, then, unless we were wise enough to begin earlier. It may also be our last chance to significantly make up for undersaving.

It's the time when our health-related patterns start digging in. Fifteen years of hard drinking and heavy smoking then can dramatically reduce both the length and quality of the second period—and of our lives in general. Conversely, that's when regular exercise, a healthy diet, and close attention to our weight and to early ailments and conditions can markedly increase the length and quality of the years to follow.

This is the time when we strengthen the bonds and friendships with our families and friends that can infuse joy and sharing in the coming Super Second Life. Links that can help create a buffer against a lonely, isolated old age.

By 55 we have also created an interest reservoir from which we can draw all the years to follow. After the frenetic sports and motion of youth, a new kind of exploration emerges during the "middle years." We find different things that we enjoy doing, seeing, hearing, reading, and trying; they whet our appetites for fuller, deeper examination and later pursuit when we have more time, fewer distractions, and less pressing responsibilities.

We begin our Super Second Life Action Plan during the "middle years."

Financially, it makes the most sense—and cents—to start promptly at 40 (if not 20) to lay out the way and means by which we can finance a comfortable later and old age. Also, to initiate the kind of lifelong health regimen that will allow us to extract from the body, and life itself, all that you wish and it can provide.

When you start your dream list and begin to plot the framework of your Super Second Life is less time-intensive. Like deciding when you will no longer be a kid, the day will come. It will speak firmly: "What am I going to do from now on?" If not sooner, I'd look for it about the time the big "5-0" falls, when pregnancy and signing that million-dollar sports contract just aren't going to happen.

But if no voice beckons, what better way to celebrate a 50+ birthday than by getting to work looking ahead on paper.

If your mind decides that it WILL NOT PLAN a Super Second Life (rebellious minds speak in capital letters), you have two choices. You can scold it firmly ("You are responsible for your own life, dummy. You're going to let others do that? Or fate?") Or don't: you'll still live on, though it may be more haphazard and less fun.

Before the First Tier: Pre-55

In an ideal world, we would spend the first 20 or so years playing and learning, the second 20 applying that learning and the lessons from that playing to developing and mastering a vocation, and the last 40 or 50 integrating all three—play, learning, and work—into a grand finale.

Yet attention must be paid to the directions and activities we early pursue, plus the kinds of relationships we develop. The wider and richer the range, the more bountiful will be the experiences and associations we can draw upon later. The more trees we firmly plant, the more abundant and varied is the fruit. The broader our companionship, the more helping hands we may offer and receive.

So when the "middle years" arrive, we have had enough experiences and known enough people to be able to make wise decisions about paths we'd like to explore more fully and people we'd like to know better as we have more time. And we have become sufficiently familiar with the educational and learning routes to be able to further investigate new ideas or trails on our own.

The Second Tier: 55 Plus

"Middle age is a period of life when one can do as much as ever but would rather not."

The only certainty of the second tier is that we arbitrarily start it after 55. It may end at 56 or 96.

The second tier closely parallel's Dr. Mary Pipher's "young-old" group in *Another Country: Navigating the Emotional Terrain of Our Elders*. I call these the "discerning years." They are the extra time given us to use the keen judgment, insight, or perception we gathered from our work, learning, and play during our first 55 years, plus any additional acumen we gather as we continue to learn and grow.

The purpose of the Action Plan is to provide guidance and intellectual support to those passing through the second and third tiers. It creates key touchpoints for those in the "discerning years," and keeps the control of their lives firmly in their hands.

The Action Plan is a rough guideline always subject to further refinement and modification. It is indeed a map to a personal territory only vaguely perceived when entered, and never fully finalized. A map in progress, it allows us to explore in any direction, filling in the details and suggested activities as it is being created and experienced.

Yet, as humans, we know about other humans who have been or are now in the land of the 55-plus. And we can project ourselves, and our wishes and dreams, on what we see and know about them. Thus planning at 40 or 50 for life at 60 or 80 is possible, though approximate.

An Action Plan that helps those 55+ maximize the use of their time, knowledge, skills, resources, and energy to enjoy a Super Second Life is what we seek.

Those in the "discerning years" will be the greatest beneficiaries if that is attained. That can bring benefits to others too: the children (and parents) of those in the "discerning years" who, like the rest of society, will see older citizens in control of full, productive lives, doing what they want to do by intent rather than happenchance, able to redesign their lives when and as they wish.

The Third Tier

The sorrow is that for most there must be a third tier, a buffer time between full independence, control and, alas, death.

> "Old age is the happiest time in a man's life. The worst of it is, there's so little of it."
>
> *William S. Gilbert*

Yet this needn't be a sad time, simply one in which we are less physically proactive and more directed to comfortably enjoying life on a daily basis.

I call these the "reflective years," the time to both think back and resonate on the achievements of a life fully lived, and to appreciate those who have been positively guided and helped by what we have done during our short earthly sojourn.

This is the period when we must call upon others to help provide support, to guide us in the areas where we have lost our independence. It is where we share what we know and have learned with our grandchildren, children, other family members, and friends.

A Super Second Life doesn't end the moment one enters this final phase of life. What one enjoyed before, they can usually, with adaptations, continue to enjoy now. The friendships gathered throughout life become more precious in the "reflective years," and often a great serenity prevails, a contentment at having done so much and been so blessed.

This is when the financial planning many years back is most appreciated, when the ability to earn is gone but costs continue. The peace at knowing that both the earlier planning and modest sacrifice now lift the burden of the costs from family, friends, or society is a particular reward of an Action Plan well executed.

So What?

Who cares if there are three or 20 tiers, and what has that to do with us?

It helps us put and keep our mental house in order by having a rational toehold on life's patterns. And it provides a logical schedule to do things when they are best done.

Tier one is when we best put the plans for a Super Second Life in motion, and adjust our actions accordingly. Tier two, the "discerning years," are when most of our active Super Second Life takes place.

Yet it's never too late to enjoy a well deserved Super Second Life. If you're 88, new to the concept and clamoring at the bit, get going!

Senescence begins
And middle age ends
The day your descendants
Outnumber your friends.

Ogden Nash

What Will You Do About Your Physical and Mental Health?

6

"If we are to believe the barrage of 'good news' dotting the press daily (about doubling our life expectancy, DNA, magic pills, and turtles that don't age), we may all live to be 200—if we can just hang on a few more weeks. So what's to worry?"

We'd better address this before we tackle present-day, flesh and bone reality!

We had also better focus on our own and our contemporaries' current and coming physical and mental health, on the long shot that corporeal immortality arrives after we've caught the last train. Without either in full temper, getting old will really be a climb to reach that leave-taking terminal.

Once we see what and where we are physically and mentally, let's implement a four-step process to gain some sense of control, in case some dreaded, adverse anomalies come knocking, uninvited and unwanted.

That is logically followed by a broader look at what physically awaits most seniors, at least in North America. There are physical ailments and conditions that appear with age. Other ailments and conditions, more opportunistic, may dash through the door the moment we open it. So we might begin a concerted campaign to hold them at bay, or remove the precursory conditions that increase the likelihood of their unwelcome entrance. Alas, some are totally out of our hands: they are gifted to us genetically. For all, this look will at least provide a pinch of understanding, to lessen the shock of seeing their new face.

A similar, broad look at our coming mental state, with its emotional and psychological components, will deal more with myths and truths than suggest steps by which we might somehow jack up our IQ another 50 points or remember our pharmacist's phone number (or location).

Then we must put all of this knowledge and information to work so we can fully use what we have to create our own very best Super Second Life. That will include synchronizing the use of our abilities while we have them to realize our dreams. Let's wait until the next chapter to create some understanding of the money and protective tools, like insurance and assistance, that we will need to be safeguarded into old old age while not being a burden on family or friends. Stress is indeed a killer; all of this may help reduce that stress.

Good health is important to a Super Second Life.

Ground rules and two myths

When we speak of a second life, aging, and health, we need a set of overriding ground rules. One, we are mortal. Two, it isn't a sin to die, but it may be not to live.

So our purpose here is to both administer and enjoy our health as well and as fully as possible so we live the best life we can.

Let's set aside two myths: old doesn't equal sick, nor, by extension, does getting older mean getting sicker. In 1994, of Americans 75-84, 73% reported no disability. Even those over 85, 40% were fully functional. And the reduction in disability is accelerating, even among those over 95.

The second is that we are all headed for the nursing home. Hardly. Only 5.2% of the populace resides in nursing homes at any one time, and while over 40% will be there at some point in their lives, many of those spend only their last days or months there before dying.

Our focus in this chapter, then, is to take a good look at our present health, how that might change as we age, and how we factor those changes into our Super Second Life plans. While disability and nursing homes might be part of those last 30 years, so will decades of full, fun living with health very much in the background. Those years are our primary concern.

"To wish to be healthy is part of being healthy."

Seneca

Of course, if our physical and mental health aren't functioning well at any age, the rest of our life directly suffers—and it may be prematurely shortened. So most of what follows are things we can do *now* to get our body, our mind, and our attitude in as good a shape as possible, so that we can fully enjoy our bonus years.

But first we should also address the "why worry?" issue, that it doesn't matter what we do, scientists are about to unveil the life-stretcher, the pill or system that will keep us all healthy and hopping until we're 200—or was that 500?—years old.

*Living to 200—
or much longer*

Live three times as long as our grandparents? A mixed blessing. Who wants to live two days longer if they are throbbing with uncontrollable, permanent pain or have the mind and future of a wrinkled potato? And who among us saved up enough survival money for two or three lifetimes?

On the other hand, with a much longer midlife and a long, enjoyable later life, given the resources and energy to do what we enjoy every day, hooray for those life-stretchers! Just think, if those 200 years were run in reverse, we'd still be able to speak with Thomas Jefferson.

But will you and I live to be 200? Fat chance. At best, we can watch with interest as science pulls forward both the fully functional length and the absolute length of life for those who follow—maybe for our grandchildren. It will be fun to watch, and if it touches us a bit, great! Right now most of us begin to suffer significant reduced function at about 70 while our absolute length is about 120.

Of course, we can already extend our lives by both paying attention to our health and by courting daily the forces that support longer life—mostly by cutting our vices and through adding a healthy diet, exercise, vigorous mental activity, and less stress (with a few magic pills thrown in). We can also hope that the forces that foster longer life appear quickly and work fast enough so we can ride their coattails. Maybe some of them will at least reverse our bodily damage—that tasted so good to inflict.

What are the changes to look for (and coattails to grab)?

- Some of the changes relate to stress, environment, and the body's ability to repair itself. Some animals don't deteriorate much at all, in safe, stressless settings. Rock fish live 150 years. We must adapt to humans what we can learn from them.

- Scientists can now double the life span of fruitflies by simply focusing on natural selection. The task is finding the genes involved, then applying pharmacology and gene replacement. When understood, reweaving the human genetic fiber will control the aging, which will allow us to stay healthier, younger, and able to fully function much longer.

- Those eating foods lower in calories, much less fat, and high in nutrients may live 1/3 longer, if animal studies on rats and monkeys hold true in humans. We will be younger physiologically and have more stamina, better immune systems, and fewer diseases, according to Drs. Rick Weindruck from the University of Wisconsin, Madison, and UCLA's Roy Walford.

- Less glucose also seems to be a longevity key, says Dr. Anthony Cerami (formerly from Rockefeller University), in part since it is also a protection against diabetes (which accelerates aging by a third). Since glucose causes harm when reacting with proteins, less glucose reduces the stiffening of joints, toughening of bones, and function loss in organs. A new compound breaks the damaging cross-linking, which is one of the causes of aging.

- Oxygen free radicals are atoms or molecules with at least one unpaired electron, and thus are usually reactive and unstable. That's bad news in humans since they are often linked to cancer. They also attack the mitochondria's membranes and thus destroy us as we age. What can we do now? According to SMU's Dr. Raj Sohal, eat fruits and vegetables and exercise!

"Health is the first wealth."

Ralph Waldo Emerson

- Dr. Miriam Nelson, from Tufts, speaks of a "magic pill," a growth hormone for use in later life to stop the loss of body strength. It will bring more muscle, less fat, and more vitality, which in turn creates a sexier, stronger, more energized person. Beware, though: one side effect is cancer.

- Turn back the aging clock? Yes, says Dr. Judith Campesi from UC. Berkeley. "If we can reset the clock in each cell by lengthening the telemeres, they can divide without limit and we can abolish aging altogether!" What happens now when the cells stop dividing? We wrinkle, our skin ages, and we can't fight disease. The solution is to restore the cells' function(s) once they stop dividing.

Are we doomed to wait for the new bullet train while riding our old coal burner until the coal runs out? Hardly.

The smartest thing we can do is what we are doing now—planning, then living the best Super Second Life possible, without losing time standing by the tracks and pining about what may be at best a mixed blessing.

Remember that our kin just a century back, at the turn of the last century, lived an average of 48 years. Hard years, without antibiotics, cars, airplanes, radio, television, the computer, aspirin, or sanitary napkins. They too dreamed of a life when most people lived to 75 and some to 100. They wondered who would benefit from such wonders. Us, that's who. Our train goes twice as far as theirs and much faster. We just have to live the journey fully.

But there's more. We can actually extend our lives today by our personal actions, by what we do, eat, and think. Let's first look at where we are now physically and mentally, then see where we can pick up some extra coal to keep our old buggies chugging a bit longer.

The status of our physical and mental health first

The first thing we have to do is determine where we are physically and mentally. Little of this is a mystery—who knows us better than ourselves? Who else feels our pains? So some of this is simply establishing a baseline, part by part, for future comparison, much as a doctor does on an initial physical exam.

To that we must add some family history, to at least be aware of areas where future attention may be drawn.

And then we must get a second opinion, in this case from our physician, to begin a life maintenance program designed to keep us healthy, active, and fully involved all our days.

The idea is to be proactive physically and mentally now, with a four-step opening volley, then include our actions into a daily regimen that is part of our lifetime maintenance program.

The first three action steps are:

(1) If it hurts, pinches, oozes, swells, or smells, **give it immediate attention**. Get it under control now; then, if possible, get it cured.
(2) If it's been lingering around and is correctable, **get it evaluated** and under treatment.
(3) If it's been around "forever" (and is chronic), **get it under control** and keep it there.

And (4), as each new health concern arises, **treat it promptly**.

The point is obvious: we should enter our Super Second Life armed with both health knowledge and a proactive plan to be able to enjoy every day fully and actively. We must get beyond the obsessive certainty that something will appear without warning and do us in. Or the worse mindset that "if I ignore it, it will go away." Either can happen, but the best armor is information, professional input, and healthy living.

So that requires a personal checklist for us to complete, then share with our physician. It can be as informal as starting with our toes and moving up, noting anything of concern now or in the past at each way station: a knee that "pops out" when we walk, a sagging libido, a lip sore that has lingered for weeks or months. Then list the senses: sight, hearing, smell, taste, and touch. Anything unusual there? We take this list to our exam and discuss each item to see if it falls into the three action categories above or if it is at the initial, flag-waving stage where subsequent changes will merit attention or treatment.

To that list we add a dozen or so categories that must also be addressed, and should be checked annually, by our physician as we age: alcohol, drug, and tobacco use and abuse; breast cancer concerns; decline in function; deconditioning; hearing problems; dental problems; high blood pressure; malnutrition; vision problems; thyroid disease; prostate disease, and depression—plus any of the others discussed later in this chapter.

The list is also incomplete without factoring in our earlier health record and our family health pattern. As well, women who have not had regular exams must include a check for cervical cancer. Those of us with significant sunlight exposure now or in the past should have a skin cancer check. Heavy drinkers and smokers should check for oral cancer. And if there are indications or family history in colon cancer or diabetes mellitus, that should be checked too. Possible coronary heart disease should make everybody's check list. And for the old old, so should obesity, dementing illness, and abuse or neglect.

A quick summary of our family's health must accompany our personal checklist when given to the doctor. Of particular concern is the health of our parents, grandparents, and siblings. What major health problems do or did they have, when did they begin, and what was the result of each. Of obvious concern are genetic hand-downs, but also a shared environment can indicate possible future health concerns we shouldn't overlook. This is not a list of impending doom but rather a peek at answers to future questions that might arise.

To our personal list and the family health record, we should add anything else of consequence in the health arena. This is the moment to clean the slate of all our preoccupations, then let our physician decide what deserves instant attention, what will be monitored, what we can do to improve our present state and keep it functioning well, and which other professionals or experts might be brought in to confront specific needs. This is also where we work with the doctor to create an ongoing, positive Super Second Life health maintenance plan. (Bring this book if your doctor has no idea what we're talking about!)

"Middle age is when a narrow waist and a broad mind begin changing places."

Glenn Dorenbush

The Appendix has a Medical Health History Questionnaire that can be completed and taken to the physician.

Why bother with all of this? Why not just live it up and take our chances later? Because by exploring our health future now, correcting the present misfunctions before they grow and worsen, and adding in the record from several generations past, we might well be able to improve our chances of a long, pain-free, active future rather than reactively having to counter whatever we are dealt.

What must we do to maintain good physical health?

It's not enough just to get a baseline evaluation. We must also put ourselves on a life-enhancing and -extending health regimen, if we want to enter and enjoy a healthy and long second life. That doesn't mean 30 years of sprouts, cold showers, and endless push-ups. But it does mean paying attention to simple, sensible acts that will make us more agile and able to do what we want longer.

One way to view this is to look backward. What are the seven habits of people who live 100+ years?

(1) sleep 7-8 hours a night
(2) eat breakfast
(3) don't eat between meals
(4) keep their weight between 5% below and 10-20% above normal for their size
(5) get regular physical activity
(6) imbibe no more than two alcoholic drinks daily
(7) don't smoke

"Life is a span of time in which the first half is ruined by our parents and the second half by our children."

And for us, who will gladly settle for most of those 100 years? We've already seen that eating food lower in calories and fat, plus favoring fruits and vegetables, are key components in programs that help eliminate free radicals and may extend our lives by a third. So one area where we can focus now and into the future is our **diet**.

Are there guidelines to determine what is a sensible diet? As many as there are nutritionists and diet-sellers. But a few have stood the tests and time. We can determine a healthy weight for ourselves (say 150 pounds), multiply that by ten, and keep our food intake within that many calories (1500), plus the number we expend in exercise (if, for example, we cycle 200 calories worth, to maintain our weight we get to ingest 1700 calories worth of food that day).

What kind of food? Keep the saturated fat a very small percentage of that total. Whole grains, fruits, and vegetables are low in calories and fat and are excellent components of any meal. We should limit our salt, and women may need more calcium and iron, before menopause. Beyond that, personal needs may require special dietary modifications. An example is the care diabetics must take to maintain proper insulin balance.

Alcohol can be a problem when used in excess. (In some, one drink is excessive.) Alcoholism in older people carries a toll, including proneness to injury (at a time when bodies mend slower and secondary complications appear), gastrointestinal illness, liver disease, malnutrition, and sometimes dementia.

Two-thirds of the chronic, excessive drinkers are longtime drinkers, but they are hardly a second life concern since most are dead by 65. At 40 we should be putting the brakes on our drinking with both feet. The other third are situational drunks; their addiction can be exacerbated by the things that age can bring, like retirement, money worries, health problems, and the death of loved ones.

There's a direct link between alcoholism, depression, and impotence, which makes it harder for alcoholics to even want to live a healthy, exciting second life, much less adhere to a healthy life style to make it happen. Women aren't excluded either; after 40, they are affected more quickly by alcohol. When should we seek help with our drinking? If the alcohol affects our relationships, influences how we schedule our days, alters our health, isolates us, or simply preoccupies us.

Exercise is very important in preventing health problems, including cardiovascular disease and depression, although less than 25% of Americans exercise at all. How beneficial? Walk an hour a day—it needn't be all at one time—and you will live two more years. Women who exercise an hour daily will cut their risk of breast cancer by a third.

Building muscle, according to Dr. Nelson, may be the most important thing older folks can do to lengthen their lives and sharpen their mental acuity. As we age, we gain weight and lose muscle strength, but the latter can be reversed in as little as two months. Simple strength and endurance exercises can be done by either sex at any age; it stops free radicals as a bonus.

The minimum goal is some type of sustained activity for 30-40 minutes at least three times a week. We needn't run marathons, scale peaks, or swim to the Azores, but the body continues to crave exercise, and it rewards us accordingly.

Dr. Mark E. Williams, in *The Complete Guide to Aging and Health*, says it best:

> Regular exercise is the best antidote to many of the effects of aging. The major benefits from regular exercise include favorable effects on fats in the blood, better handling of blood sugar, increased maximal oxygen capacity, greater strength, denser bones, an improved sense of well-being, and better sleep.

Smoking has deservedly received a bum health rap these past years, and anybody who doesn't know that it is harmful to their health probably *is* one of those aliens we see in movies living in human bodies. So if we're resisting with all of our might, puffing into our second life is a luxury we can ill afford. In a nutshell: it's far more likely to painfully shorten than extend those extra years.

Alas, the body is more forgiving than society. Quit now and in two to five years our elevated risk of heart disease is about equal to a non-smoker. The risks of cancer and emphysema also drop markedly. Circulation improves. Friends return. Insurance rates drop. And we aren't reminded daily that cigarette smoking remains the single most preventable cause of death in the United States for men and women and that we can cure 85% of all cancer if people (like us) stopped smoking.

The last thing we can do to extend our life and make it more enjoyable is to reduce our **stress**. Stress is the body's response to a demand, and too much stress has physical and psychological consequences, including insomnia, headaches, and ulcers. It wears the body down and reduces the amount of repair the body makes to itself, which induces aging.

There are solutions—and good news: we experience less stress as we age! We can simply stop worrying so often, at least about things over which we have no control. Earthquakes, conspiracies, the falling ruble, even bad jokes happen but beyond taking prudent precautions and remaining attentive, the stress we develop about them and other uncontrollable actions serve no useful purpose. Healthy coping mechanisms to stress include exercise, meditation, biofeedback, or self-hypnosis; unhealthy ones include overeating and substance abuse.

What you are doing now—planning a full, active, enjoyable Super Second Life—may be the very best way to reduce stress. You are taking control and creating your own future reality. Since you are the creator, if things don't work out, no stress—just change the reality!

Living long enough to enjoy a Super Second Life does have health consequences beyond those just mentioned. Everyday things change because of age. These are the most common examples that we must consider now and factor into our future plans:

- The third addiction (after tobacco and alcohol) is **drugs**. Not many dedicated cocaine or heroin users reach middlessence. A bigger concern are the old-fashioned, doctor-prescribed legal drugs. Not every user is addicted and some simply must use them to live those extra years with any pleasure, but the guess is that about 60% of the 50+ users are needlessly addicted to painkillers, tranquilizers, sedatives, sleeping pills, or muscle relaxants.

- Let's look at **depression** again because it is so common in seniors and is an organic illness with biochemical changes in the body. It's estimated that 25% of the seniors dip into depression at some point, and that 1/3 of those with dementia probably are depressed and are treatable. The treatment for depression is specific drugs and psychotherapy, one or

"Life is a game that must be played."

Edwin Arlington Robinson

both. Sometimes it passes on its own in six months—but what a lousy, hopeless six months. Dangerous too, because the depressed can turn to suicide. Particularly vexing to seniors is the depression created by mixing alcohol with specific allergy medicines, antidepressants, barbiturates, motion sickness medication, painkillers, sleeping pills, and some blood pressure prescriptions.

- Let's talk **sex**, again. It can be a vital element of a Super Second Life, or so thought 97% of 800 folks 60-91 years old in a study that said they liked sex. Eighty percent thought it was good for their health. But **impotence** can soften that enthusiasm real fast! Yet 50-60% of the 10 million men thus afflicted have a physical cause that can be treated. Prescription drugs can be one of those possible causes. There are 41 that can be implicated, including Tagamet, Desyrel, Prozac, and Valium—plus, of course, alcohol and tobacco.

- **Prostate enlargement** starts appearing in the 40s and will be present in virtually all men by about 65. Three things to consider: (1) get a PSA blood test often to make sure it doesn't become cancerous; (2) exercise and sex help in the short run ("Head for the bed, Mabel. My prostate's acting up!"), and (3) there are effective drugs now to use before or instead of surgery.

- If we can keep our **heart** in shape, bingo—that's the #1 killer in folks over 50. So we need to get our blood pressure checked and treated if it's too high, watch our cholesterol levels, pay attention to our diet (or start one) if we're more than 20% over our ideal body weight, and exercise regularly.

- **Menopause** used to be a hint to get coffin insurance. Now women live a third of a great life with and after menopause. Some see it as the gateway to an exciting new beginning, but the passing can be unpleasant: 75% of the women have symptoms. Most are immediately treatable. Menopause can also create a new, positive, dynamic in a marriage. It's also

"Middle age is when you are not inclined to exercise anything but caution."

Arthur Murray

a time to see your physician—to see if hormone replacement therapy is for you and learn more about preventing osteoporosis.

- Women jump into the fore for **heart disease** after menopause, so weight is an issue. Attention to eating matched with exercise can usually remove this concern.

- What fun is a second life if we're as blind as Magoo? By 45, most of us need corrective lenses; almost all do by 60. So we need to get our **eyes** checked, in part for macular degeneration. (While there, have a glaucoma check. Two million people have it and half don't know.) If cataracts are found, 95% of those with them had improved vision after surgery. And forget tinted lenses or sunglasses at night after we're 60: we need seven times the light that a 20 year-old requires. There are also amazing laser eye surgeries that quickly correct near- and far-sightedness.

- If our **hearing** is getting worse, guess what, it happens with age, mostly to men. (A quick cure: move to the African Sudan, where there is no hearing loss.) Unfortunately, the range most affected includes the human voice. The single greatest cause? Excessive earwax! Some need surgery or earwax irrigation; most use hearing aids. We could also learn lip reading if we weren't so blind!

- Most of us grew up on the edge of the fluoride revolution in dentistry, so we're still likely candidates for cavities as well as **periodontal disease**. Ninety percent of us will be affected by the latter, giving true meaning to "long in the tooth!" The best advice: brush twice daily, floss, and visit the dental hygienist at least once a year. The goal is to keep all of the teeth we can and stay pain free.

- **Arthritis** is what most people think of when they think of aging. Gnarled paws, inflamed knees, and massive aspirin-popping! For 17% of us, that's about it. Most people get it when they're younger and it gets progressively worse and chronic, which needn't be. Some arthritis can be stopped in its tracks if found early enough; most can be managed and permanent disabilities prevented. The form most commonly seen is rheumatoid arthritis, which appears in our 30s and 40s. Aspirin is still the wonder drug. But osteoarthritis comes from the gradual disintegration of cartilage. We get it early but feel it in our 50s. Keeping our weight down, exercising, and regular stretching are helpful. Keeping in contact with our physician makes sense here to stay current with the wonders taking place in pharmacology and genetic treatment.

"The spiritual eyesight improves as the physical eyesight declines."

Plato

- **Diabetes** is a major concern as we age. It's an endocrine disorder that requires strict attention to diet and lifestyle. There are two kinds. The one that is new to seniors is the maturity-onset diabetes, affecting 14 million Americans. It usually appears after 40 and is controllable, mostly by diet and exercise. The affected do not need insulin but must pay strict attention to a treatment regimen to reduce disability that generally affects the eyes and limbs. Over 80% are overweight when diagnosed. We should always get tested for diabetes at our regular exam.

- If diabetes isn't the greatest fear of seniors, then surely **Alzheimer's disease** is. While it's not as prevalent as we think (at the most, four million have it or a similar form of dementia), it is devastating in the loss of memory and function to the person and the violent disruption it makes in the lives of their families. It usually appears in the 60s, is psychologically devastating in its early stages, and survival is generally less than five years. There is no known cure at present.

These are the factors to consider when we establish a Super Second Life baseline with our doctor. What problems or conditions we have now, what might we expect in the future based on our family history, and what our lifestyle might inflict upon us. This proactive knowledge, with a program to confront each need as it arises, puts more control of our future in our hands.

What must we do to maintain good mental health?

Taking control of our lives may also be the single most important thing we can do to develop and maintain our own mental well-being. Being in control silences helplessness and despair, the true foes of age.

It's important to know that while we will slow down, functionally we won't be much different mentally in 30 years than we are now. We have no more reason to fear instant insanity or sudden senility than we do to expect our hands to suddenly turn green.

Senior mental health isn't an oxymoron nor do all consider aging as synonymous with mental decrepitude. In China, where age is honored, the elderly perform much higher on tests than their American counterparts.

Granted, some seniors are dithering, bewildered, and uncertain who or where they are, but most of those are very old and or very sick—and some aren't seniors at all! A third of us will function as well as ever at least into our 80s, and almost all of the rest will follow a slow, predictable path of sanity at a slower pace through our second lives.

As we saw earlier in Chapter 1, we will lose the ability to perform some mental exercises quickly. We will perform simple tasks slower, and worse if they are complex or we are surprised. (Some of that has nothing to do with the mind. We are stiffer and more afraid to do them wrong.) Our short-term memory will get poorer and we won't be able to skunk the young in such things as typing and list memorization. And in times of severe stress or major loss, we might mentally freeze up for a while. It sounds awful but we will persevere.

We'll do so because the tests that measure those dwindling capacities don't test all of the experiential knowledge and skills we gathered, including the pesky ability of older people to improvise, compensate, and unconsciously create tricks to be able to think and function just as fast (or nearly so) as our younger counterparts. Other tests show that other kinds of memory, like the procedural memory of how to play golf or swim, aren't touched by age at all.

It wasn't a total surprise, then, when a test group in Seattle, completing the same complete battery of tests every seven years, didn't steadily decline in their cognitive abilities after they passed 20. In fact, in skills that counted, they stayed about the same until they were in their 60s. Only by their 80s were there some areas of significant loss.

Who held up the best? Well educated, middle class, healthy, flexible people. The most important trait? Flexibility. In fact, Dr. K. Warner Schaie, from Penn State, who designed the Seattle Longitudinal Study, found mental flexibility—the willingness to improvise and to try unorthodox ways of doing things—a prime predictor of mental vivacity in the later years. Conversely, the more mentally rigid the person became as they aged and the lower their satisfaction with life, the quicker the deterioration of their intellect.

Schaie identified the three factors most often associated with strong mental function in older age groups to be an above-average level of education, a complex and stimulating lifestyle, and being married to a smart spouse.

"Life is a series of inspired follies. The difficulty is to find them to do. Never lose a chance: it doesn't come every day."

George Bernard Shaw

Other studies show that we gain in wisdom as we accumulate life experiences and we also improve in our ability to manage our daily affairs. In fact, when tested in offering advice about fundamental matters of life, older people consistently knocked the socks off of their younger counterparts.

Our mental slippage is not due to loss of brain cells, which myth suggests die out 100,000 at a time. Rather, they remain in the brain but become senescent, or dormant, according to Harvard's Dr. Gerald Fischbach. What's more important is that there is very little loss in the cortex, where elaborate thinking takes place.

Our best hope now is two-pronged. First, we can stop this loss by helping the neurons survive. Free radicals are part of the problem, but so are stress hormones, which will do damage if elevated for too long. All of us, then, can reduce our stress. And women after menopause can take estrogen, since that helps increase dendrites and regrow cells. The benefit? It will help restore their verbal memory and cognitive performance.

"By the time a man gets to green pastures, he can't climb the fence."

And we can train our brain to learn again. Older brains have an astonishing ability to rejuvenate themselves, but they do it by rewiring the neurons. Studies find tutoring can recover all that was lost in the past—it was still there when retested seven years later! Even the memorization of random numbers and names. Even to prevent dementia, brain exercise and vigorous use is recommended.

Our greatest fear is that at some point we will totally lose our mental function. How would we care for ourselves or make life-sustaining decisions? Again, Dr. Mark Williams addresses this:

> For most of us this fear of becoming mentally incompetent is groundless. Much harm results from the assumption that all mental functions decline with age. We begin to believe the stereotype, which encourages us to withdraw and lose our self-esteem. Mental function does not have to decline; the capacity to learn continues through life.

Current studies of the mind and aging show four things we can do to maintain and even increase our brain power almost as long as we live:

(1) Maintain good health and a strong cardiovascular system
(2) Seek intellectual enrichment
(3) Exercise
(4) Control our lives

Let's look at each of these to see how they might help us restructure our activities in our Super Second Life.

Good health and a strong cardiovascular system

There's no absolute correlation between a sound body and a sound mind although sickness clearly saps energy from and redirects a mind. There is a link, though, between those with heart disease, diabetes, and high blood pressure and mental decline. It's as likely to be the lifestyles that lead to both the physical and mental impairments as the diseases themselves: overeating, inactivity, and stress.

Memory loss is neither inevitable nor untreatable. Harvard neurologists are finding that later in life the brain stops producing a hormone involved in memory. So memory boosters are on the horizon: a dozen other substances are also candidates, including psychoactive drugs that could mimic the missing chemical and reinvigorate the memory.

Keeping us mentally sharp seems as simple as undertaking a variety of new, enjoyable, challenging activities. That seems to force the brain to actually grow.

Intellectual enrichment is good for the brain

Old rats provided the clue to how this happens. UC. Berkeley's Dr. Marian Diamond gave toys to some rats, none to others. The neurons of the rats with the new challenge quickly sprouted new connections that enlarged the blood flow to their brains. Brains with more connections have a higher cognitive capacity. They may also resist Alzheimer's.

There were two more conclusions for humans, since the effect on rats diminished when the novelty wore off and they grew bored. So we too must vary our mental stimuli. And it won't continue if we don't "enjoy" the activity.

What might we read here? If we don't do something at least as exciting after retirement as before, we will lose ground. If we don't consciously seek something relatively new and agreeable or gratifying, we won't be keeping our mind refreshed. And if we don't plan for new and challenging activities, they probably won't happen.

Exercise gets blood to the brain

We saw earlier the benefits of exercise for the body, young or old. It logically follows that the brain, being a bodily organ, would also benefit.

Science has now proven the point. In tests, humans who exercised did better in cognition and mental performance. The exercise increased the blood supply to their brains, elevated the brain's own chemicals, and brought oxygen and antioxidants. Tests in rats showed the same result: the brains of rats that exercised increased in cognition, learning, and motor skills. Their brains were more active and in better health.

Alas, more is not better. Thirty minutes a day of walking is far better than no exercise at all. But hours of exercise in older test subjects shows diminishing results.

Life satisfaction is important too

Why would liking life and being emotionally balanced be just as influential on the aging mind as mental activity? We know that those who suffer from negative emotions like depression, anxiety, and anger score lower than those who find life satisfying.

Dr. Robert Sapolsky, from Stanford, may have the answer. His theory is that the stress-related release of adrenal hormones bathes neurons in a dangerous chemical wash that can eventually damage the brain.

Knowing what's coming strengthens our mental health

An important study published in 1972 by James H. Barrett lets us see how our mental and emotional health is challenged during our second life, and what we can do to preserve our stability and confront the changes.

He sees six major regressive tasks confronting the elderly.

See Barrett, James H., **Gerontological Psychology** *(Thomas, 1972).*

(1) accepting and adjusting to a decline in physical health, the onset of which can be delayed by a good balanced diet, regular check-ups, and exercise.
(2) adjusting to a reduction in sexuality, in part related to changes in sex drive and the physical debilitation of their spouse.
(3) readjustment to their dependent-independent pattern of living.
(4) acceptance of a different role in the family.
(5) learning to accept more than they can give.
(6) reorientation to their primary social group.

Are we all subject to these six major changes? If we live long enough, probably. But an independent, well planned life and a supportive family can delay most of them, and make the emotional transition natural and gradual.

Barrett suggests seven compensatory tasks that should help us meet these changes and make a better adjustment in old age.

The first is what this book is all about: **develop new leisure time activities to meet changing abilities and financial limitations**. We go farther on these pages by helping us identify those financial limitations, abilities, and dreams. We then try to optimally match them so that we can live the best life possible when the expenditure of that energy, ability, and funds makes the most sense.

Learn new work skills. This is particularly important to those who must or want to continue working.

The third, **readjust dietary needs**, acknowledges that we need a healthy but different diet as we age.

Adjust to changing environments recognizes that aging usually requires differing housing accommodations, often in new locales.

> "Growing old is no more than a bad habit which a busy man has no time to form."
>
> *André Maurois*

A hard change is to **adjust to the changing mores of society**. Every new generation has a new set of rules, music, and standards. Live and let live seems to work best here. We needn't hum rap music any more than the new set must dance the bunny hop or do the twist.

The sixth says that we must **adjust to a new status or role in society**. We're no longer top dogs; others are running the companies, community, and clubs. But we can still be vital participants and even acquire a new, different status through our new activities, if that's what we want.

The most important may be the seventh: **change your individual self-concept**. We must find a comfortable new us that will withstand the buffeting winds of a new world. We must be pleased with who we are and which of our values we want to project into our second lives. Again, by defining a Super Second Life and what is important to us, we are defining that self-concept, plus creating the ways we will live it in the years to come.

Joanne M. Schrof's article in the *U.S. News & World Report* (Nov. 28, 1994) provides excellent suggestions of what we might do at various stages of our life to stay mentally vital as we age.

- In childhood, eat properly (to avoid nutritional deficits that can permanently impair mental functions), get lots of stimulation (which can increase brain cell connections by as much as 25%), and stay in school.
- In young adulthood, make many friends, find a mentor (to get older adults' advice), marry someone smarter than you, and take adult courses (but don't cram).
- In middle age, develop expertise, save money (so you can afford mind-nourishing experiences), achieve your major goals then (so you don't enter retirement unfulfilled), and avoid burnout.
- After 65, seek new horizons, resist the temptation to settle into a comfy routine, engage the world (do things you believe make a difference in life), take a daily walk, and keep control (helplessness leads to mental apathy and deterioration).

Our biggest danger isn't loss of mental function but of just giving up, of saying "it's too late" or "why try?" This is called "disengagement," and it strikes too often shortly after retirement, when we have fewer interactions with colleagues and they are less rewarding. We're the odd person out, and the eventual result is withdrawal and isolation. It marches in hand with depression.

Its prevention and cure seem to be the same: finding and maintaining a sense of well-being, a kind of ongoing purposefulness. An examination at our lives, finding them different but acceptable. Good health also helps—plus a positive outlook and a satisfaction with life in general.

Did you ever notice that those seniors who flat-out enjoy life are having most of the fun? And there's a lot more of them around? And they live to a ripe old age? We might look for a clue there.

Planning our Super Second Life can help too. By forming a future where we build on those elements we want to share with others, we not only keep actively involved in continuously creating our own fate, it allows us to define our future role in work, our family, and our chosen social group. It's the antithesis of withdrawal.

Synchronizing our desires with our abilities

"The great use of life is to spend it for something that outlasts us."

William James

Why do we bother to do all of this? Granted, we can slow things down a bit by capping the booze and exercising—even switching from Big Macs to Little Macs. But isn't the idea to have fun in the second life, not to be forced to count calories and see if Aunt Tess had a bum ticker?

You got it! To have fun; contribute again; contribute differently; find joy, then spread it to others.

Getting a handle on our health now and taking simple, straightforward steps to retain our vigor and abilities as long as possible is why we need both a baseline and a set of guidelines for future healthy living.

It also helps us better fill in our time pegs so that we realize our dreams when we have the capacity to fully enjoy and accomplish them.

What does that mean?

That if we want to hike 500 miles on the Appalachian Trail and we have an ankle tendon that's been acting up, we do three things: get the tendon tended to, train up on several shorter weekend treks, and schedule our major hike when we are young and vigorous enough to enjoy it.

Common sense? You'd think so until you talk to every other senior with plans a decade too late to perform.

It means first creating that Super Second Life health maintenance program with our physician. Determining what we must attend to immediately, what must be evaluated, how and when those treatments will take place, which chronic problems we must get under control, and how that affects our activities.

To that we add the changes we are making in our daily lives to make them healthier. And we factor in those things from our family history that may or will require attention in the future, with as many details as we and our doctor can conjure.

All of these factors are projected on a 30-year map to see in which 5-year or 10-year time pegs we will best be able to do the things we want. Some of it is absolute: we can't hike until the ankle is healed. Some is approximate: we'd like to lose ten pounds before we take part in an Elderhostel dig. Some is indeed common sense: getting our pilot's license is a sooner rather than later thing, in part because of the family's propensity to go bat blind as they age. And some is situational: we don't want to plan much for the next year because of the progressively worsening health of a terminal parent.

So we need this information for our Action Plans explained in Chapter 14.

And we need this information to lead a sensible life at any age. Since we are mortal and mortals die, we simply need it to live the best we can.

Health Sources

Barrett, James H., *Gerontological Psychology* (Thomas, 1972).

Ettinger, Walter H., M.D., and Brenda S. Mitchell, Ph.D., and Steven N. Blair, PED, *Fitness After 50* (Cracom Publications, 1996). Sensible.

Rosenfeld, Isadore, M.D., *Live Now Age Later* (Warner Books, 1999).

Rowe, John. W., M.D., and Robert L. Kahn, Ph.D., *Successful Aging: The MacArthur Foundation Study* (Dell, 1998).

Williams, Mark E., M.D., *The American Geriatrics Society's Complete Guide to Aging and Health* (Harmony Books, 1995). An excellent, no-nonsense guide.

For a list of aging-related health organizations (with address, phone, and website), please see the Appendix.

I have made it a rule to go to bed when there wasn't anybody left to sit up with; and I have made it a rule to get up when I have to... In the matter of diet, I have been persistent in sticking to the things which didn't agree with me until one or the other got the best of it. For thirty years I have taken coffee and bread at eight in the morning and no bite nor sup until seven-thirty in the evening... I have made it a rule never to smoke more than one cigar at a time... I smoke in bed until I have to go to sleep; I wake up in the night, sometimes once, sometimes twice, sometimes three times, and I never waste any of these opportunities to smoke... As for drinking, I have no rule about that. When the others drink, I like to help; otherwise I remain dry, by habit and preference... Since I was seven years old I have seldom taken a dose of medicine, and have still seldomer needed one... I have never taken any exercise, except sleeping and resting, and I never intend to take any. Exercise is loathsome. And it cannot be any benefit when you are tired; and I was always tired.

Mark Twain

Money and Your Super Second Life

7

If the retirement financial gurus are to be believed, a chunk of our first dollar (or newborn rattle)—and every cent since—should be immediately banked so it can compound for our assuredly shaky and most likely disastrous economic future!

Their claims are mostly overblown and their predictions far too dire, but there are sensible reasons why the young should start thinking about and saving for their later years, so it isn't a heavy pecuniary burden while they are young nor are there any needs or options unmeetable when they age. Reasons too why we should get our present spending and saving under better control.

This chapter looks realistically at money and the Super Second Life. Its purpose is to help us best use our available budget to achieve the most satisfying and rewarding Super Second Life. It will send us to other books listed at the end of the chapter for their expert formulae, strategies, and techniques designed to help us create the kind of savings and growth investments needed to free us up from second life financial concerns.

Here we are far more interested in what we want to do with that money. How it will help us realize our second life dreams. Otherwise, we're all madly gathering goods, instead of living now, without any idea of why we want them or what they are for.

We need to take a hard look at where our present assets are and what they amount to, plus what those might be worth in coming times. As well, we need to see how we create our income and how we spend it. And we need a flexible Money Worksheet that we can use later (and throughout our life) to see how and when we can finance our future dreams. So charts we will see—and use.

Four components of our overall financial plan deserve comment too: the basics, emergencies, how long we plan to work, and our will. Then 26 guidelines plucked from the best financial planning minds, distilled, and offered to help create a fully affordable Super Second Life.

Money is also important to a Super Second Life.

The old system doesn't make much sense

The conventional money approach to "getting ready for the future" or "saving up for our old age" doesn't make much sense—work like maniacs in our big-bucks years, save a bundle, retire, spend it as slowly as possible, hope to die instantly and painlessly, then leave a pile (plus our old clothes) to our kids.

What's missing from that picture? Us, humans with hearts. And real lives—but only one life per person, at least in this world, and if there's a later world all that money is irrelevant, if not a black mark.

Somewhere the purpose of life gets lost in the conventional approach. Without a larger purpose to all that working, saving, pinching, and willing, we become automatons going through the paces, ciphers adding and subtracting ciphers.

Breathtaking sunsets, hearing your first song performed, dropping a birdie on the third hole, selling buildings or bread, watching your kids (or kids' kids) hook a bluegill, and helping Habitat for Humanity roof a home—or reading, running, designing a patio, or ushering at church—all disappear unless we have a grander vision of why we are here and what the human miracle is all about.

"Money is like an arm or a leg—use it or lose it."

Henry Ford

At 40 or 50, the real issue isn't whether we have amassed enough money to live as we wish, but whether we know what we need the money for, have enough to realize our dreams

74

(plus enough in reserve for unexpected surprises), and know how much we want left when we die.

It's drawing up a plan for the rest of our life, then matching our present and future resources to it and making it come true.

Drawing up that grander plan, mainly defining and accomplishing the dreams, is what this book is about.

Looking at the major financial concerns is the purpose of this chapter.

These pages don't tell you how to make money, save, buy stocks or bonds, invest, or even spend, although they may touch on most of those. There are scores of other books by financial experts that dwell on each topic. Here we focus on a second life plan and how money fits in.

The two are distinct. We will all have a second life, unless fate ordains otherwise. That much is free. It comes with the human territory. But we won't all have the same amount of money, and some of us will have very, very little. Wherever we are on the resources scale, a Super Second Life nonetheless involves living our latter days as fully and enjoyably as possible.

Rich or poor, we all get to look at and enjoy the same lush meadows and midday sun. We can dream, of jousting, juggling, or talking with kings. We can pray and sing and construct. We can read and write and compose. We can invent, share, and teach.

And, as noted, we all get second lives. We don't need to plan or save to have Super Second Lives, but it sure helps. The planning lets us do more things at appropriate times. And having some dispensable cash, plus some fall-back reserves, gives us many more choices.

In Part Two of this book we will design the kind of Super Second Life we want, and create an Action Plan broken into time-pegs so we will have a rough idea of when we will need specific inputs of money to make our dreams come true.

Here we must discuss, in broad terms, the basics we need to live a decent life: shelter, food, clothing, transportation, medical expenses, and so on. Plus an emergency contingency to weather extraordinary costs or just to dip into in hard times.

"Money is something that talks. Most of us can't keep it long enough to hear what it says."

Jimmy Lyons

We must also look at how long we intend to create income. Will we flee the work force the moment we qualify for retirement? Fold our tent at 65? Work whenever we want spot cash? Or keep our foot in the employment camp almost forever?

And what is our post-life goal? Are we gathering it all up just so we can have it distributed (after taxes) to our children who outlive us? Or would we rather spend and distribute it before the harps start strumming?

A final thought before we look at the particulars.

There can be a strong argument in favor of "working like a maniac and saving up a bundle in our first life," if we substitute "hard" for "like a maniac." But only if that earning fervor is matched by other, equally important concerns: getting a solid education, having as many quality growth and vocational experiences as possible, building a corps of supportive friends, and creating a rich personal life. All while identifying those characteristics you want to exemplify and have associated with your name, like honesty, integrity, dependability, perseverance, and trust.

Only a minute, enlightened few have an overriding life plan when we're young. Most of us barely have a plan for next Tuesday. We're creatures of nature, as we saw in Chapter 4. We're finding out who we are and what's important. Hard work can be a valuable component of that search, and saving is a huge plus, in part because of what it says about our ability to know, prioritize, and discipline our desires. It also gives us choices later on, when our working vigor may be less. And it moves us from having to rely on fate, by putting our future as well as the present more into our own economic hands.

So if we've been working and saving and are now thinking about the coming years, we simply have more beans to count, shuffle, and spend. How many beans? Let's see.

What we have now and may have later

There's something ethereal about discussing finances without knowing what we have in the coffers. So now's the time to do a tally, then some projections so we can guesstimate where we will be at some arbitrarily critical points in our future.

First we must see what we have available in income, then what our expenditures are. From that we can create a Super

Second Life Money Worksheet. All can be done annually or for specific time periods.

Completing each now serves as a baseline for our calculations both in Part Two of this book and to use in seeing how much separates us, financially, now from where we'd like to be at certain points in the future. Past income tax forms are helpful in making these calculations.

Copy the forms that follow, if you wish...

Super Second Life Money Worksheet: Year or Age			
Annual basic living expenses		(A)	$
Annual basic income:			
Annual Social Security income	$		
Annual pension income	$		
Other annual income: Royalties	$		
Other annual income:	$		
Other annual income:	$		
Total income	(add totals above)	(B)	$
Annual basic income deficit/surplus	(A) - (B)	(C)	$
Monthly supplemental income needed	÷12		$
Special super life expenses this year	(from Action Plan)	(D)	$
Total money desired for this year	(A) + (D)		$
Maximum income deficit/surplus	if C is -, (C) + (D)		
	if C is +, (C) - (D)	(E)	$
Monthly supplemental income needed	÷12		$
Additional income source(s):	Amount		
Income source:	$		
Income source:	$		
Income source:	$		
Income source:	$		
Income source:	$		
Income source:	$		
Income source:	$		
Income source:	$		
Income source:	$		
Income source:	$		
Income source:	$		
Additional income available this year	$	(F)	
Total income deficit/surplus for this year	C + F		$

77

Super Second Life Income Worksheet: Year or Age—					
INCOME	Annual	Monthly	Begins in Year	Ends in Year	Reserve
Social Security	$	$			$
Retirement benefits					
Disability benefits					
Survivor's benefits					
Pension plans					
Employer					
Voluntary (IRA, Roth, 401[k], Keogh)					
Veteran's benefits					
Interest					
Dividends					
Early retirement bonus					
Insurance payments					
Life insurance					
Health insurance					
Long-term care insurance					
Disability insurance					
Conversion of personal investments					
Retirement savings					
General savings					
Property and goods					
Mutual funds					
Treasury bills					
Stocks					
Bonds					
Certificates					
Annuities					
Loans receivable					
Inheritances					
After-death inheritance					
Living inheritance (cash gift transfers)					
Working Income					
Full-time employment					
Part-time job:					
Part-time job:					
Self-employment income					
Residual income (royalties)					

What Are You Going to Do With Your Extra 30 Years?

INCOME (2)	Annual	Monthly	Begins in Year	Ends in Year	Reserve
In-kind income (companion, house tender)	$	$			$
Home income					
Rental income					
Sale income					
Reverse mortgage					
Rental / sale of other real estate					
Gift income					
Personal holdings					
Sale of personal possessions					
Sale of collectibles					
Sale of car, boat, trailer, camper, etc.					
Other sales					
Use of emergency fund					
TOTAL INCOME	$	$			$

Super Second Life Expense Worksheet: Year or Age—					
EXPENSES	Annual	Monthly	Begins in Year	Ends in Year	Reserve
House payment or rent	$	$			$
Maintenance					
Furnishing					
Improvements					
Property tax					
Food					
Utilities					
Water					
Electricity					
Gas					
Oil					
Trash / Sewage					
Other:					
Inflation (2-3% a year)					
Phone					
Computer costs					
Clothing					

What Are You Going to Do With Your Extra 30 Years?

EXPENSES (2)	Annual	Monthly	Begins in Year	Ends in Year	Reserve
Purchases	$	$			$
Cleaning					
Health costs					
Care					
Medicine					
Taxes					
Federal					
State					
Local					
Self-employment					
Transportation					
Car payments					
Gas, oil, repairs					
Parking					
Commuting / public transportation					
Professional fees					
Gifts and donations					
Loan repayments					
Loan debts					
Personal care					
Care of family members or dependents					
Education					
Exercise / Fitness					
Travel / Vacation					
Savings investment					
Emergency fund					
Hobby costs					
Pets					
Entertainment					
Divorce costs (alimony, child support)					
Interest: credit card and other					
Assumed debts: children/others					
Insurance: Health					
Auto					
Property					
Life					
Disability					
Liability					
TOTAL EXPENSES	$	$			$

Super Second Life Net Worth Worksheet: Year or Age—					
NET WORTH	Now	1 Year	5 Years	10 Years	15 Years
Assets					
Checking account(s)	$	$	$	$	$
Savings account(s)					
Bond(s)					
Certificate(s)					
Market value of home/apartment					
Market value of other real estate					
IRA and Keogh plans					
Cash value of life insurance					
Surrender value of annuities					
Equity in profit-sharing / pension plans					
Market value of stocks					
Market value of bonds					
Market value of mutual funds					
Current value of car(s)					
Current value of household furnishings and appliances					
Current value of furs and jewelry					
Loans receivable					
Other assets					
Total Assets (A)	$	$	$	$	$
Liabilities					
Mortgage balance	$	$	$	$	$
Loans: auto					
Loans: student					
Loans: home equity					
Current bills					
Credit-card balance					
Other debts:					
Total Liabilities (B)	$	$	$	$	$
Current Net Worth (A) minus (B)	$	$	$	$	$

How much should we have saved?

"Money is an eel in the hand."

Welsh proverb

Super Second Life money

Who knows? If we need a heart attack, simply do the calculations in most of the books cited at the end of this chapter. It's seldom under $1,000,000, often two or three times that. And if you didn't start saving at seven, you'd better clone a second you earning full income to catch up!

Don't panic. We all agree that a regular savings program begun early makes huge sense later on. That 401(k) and similar programs are super. Pensions are a blessing. Even IRAs are fine. That what might save our bacon is compounded interest, the longer to compound the better.

If we had just been as brilliant in our wild days as we are now, reading this book, we'd know why we want this windfall and it would be a lot easier to make modest sacrifices to make those future dreams come true. But we didn't, and even if we had read these words at 25, or maybe even 40, we would probably have laughed our immortal laugh and said, "Later, I'm too busy living now."

We won't starve to death. We won't have to live under bridges. But we may have to trim our dream sails to match a lesser wind.

It's never too late to lead a Super Second Life, and if our lack of savings means that we have to keep working a bit longer or settle for a trip to Tulsa instead of Tahiti, there we are. (Too humid in Tahiti anyway.) What's most important now is when we'll need special jets of money to brighten up our later days.

In Part Two we will define the dreams that will highlight our second life. Most of them cost money, so we will use the numbers in the Super Second Life Money Worksheet, estimate the cost of those second life dreams, and plug them all into the appropriate time pegs in our Action Plan.

How do we know now how much money we must save and earn to do what we want with at least some comfort and security? We don't, and we won't really know until then. For one thing, we may die first. (That's a tough way to save money.) Or what costs a dollar now may cost ten then (or 40 cents). Or we may have a vastly different concept of that dream then than now. So putting future price tags on dreams is very hard.

There's another point, too. If we don't have the funds at that time, we just won't do it, or we'll do the part of the dream we can afford, or we'll do it vicariously (which should be free). Or we may come out of "retirement" (again) and work long enough to muster up the mammon.

What's more vexing than trying to financially plan without numbers? Have patience. There's no rush. Some of these activities are 20 or 30 years away.

The basics

Alas, the basics aren't 20 or 30 years off. They are here and now, and will be every day of our lives. So they must be factored in at each step. Shelter, food, clothing, transportation, medical expenses, and so on.

Until we hit our second life, at say 55, figure that what we are spending now for everyday living (emergencies aside) is what we will need in the bridge years, plus a bit more for inflation. If we upgrade our life style, the cost of basics rises.

But we get a break later. It costs less to be a senior. Figure our needs at that time at from 60-75% of our present costs, with 70% the number usually given.

Why does it cost less? We will eat a bit less, entertain less and less grandly, probably quit smoking, drink less and less often, drive older cars longer, get discounts almost everywhere, buy fewer new clothes, have fewer high-priced toys, and—hear a huge sigh of relief—no longer have to feed, clothe, medicate, and in general support kids!

Emergencies

At any stage of our adult lives it is prudent to have at least six months of full earning set aside in a compounding emergency fund. That is no less important as we age.

The fund can cover a dozen calamities in our youth, and is a substitute bread winner should we become disabled, to tide us over until disability insurance or other forms of back-up support kick in. It also pays the bills between jobs, relieving the panic of having to accept any job at any rate just to feed mouths and pay rent.

But as we enter our second life, an emergency fund often meets two key needs: loss from job income and to pay non-insured medical expenses, including nursing home costs. In later years, we can also supplement Social Security income from the interest it earns.

*How long do
we plan to work?*

When almost all work was back-breaking and only the hardy survived to 65, retirement was a blessed goal. But in today's economy, the Social Security one can earn at 65 (or a few years later as the collection year is moved up) can pay for about 40% of our needs. (For the rich, this may be as low as 25%. For those with a very modest income, it can be as much as 70%.) The age that we stop working may largely be dependent upon whether we have been able to gather the remaining percent of our current income needed to fill the gap to the 70% or so we will later require.

Add to that 70% any expensive desires in our Super Second Life, or any grand leap in the cost of the basics, and our choice of leaving some tangent of the work world may not be ours at all.

There are also those who simply enjoy working—it's called "play for play." Some of us will want to be fully employed until they bronze us and put us in the hall. Others will seek part-time employment, and still others, as-needed jobs.

And how many are gnawing at the bit to leave the conventional workforce to start our own latter-life company? Or become consultants? Or work-at-home spot job independents? Or supertemps? Or authors in print?

Not included in the above are the thousands of volunteer positions, some of which have perks with economic value, like special discounts and free meals.

So when we stop working is based on many factors, not the least of which is how we see working as part of our Super Second Lives. For some of us, it will be an integral element that we will plan around. It may be the vehicle that will get us abroad, after which we will attach a month of leave to enjoy the locale. Or we may work in the summer when the tourists come calling, and go visit them the rest of the year. We may work the ski season or when the ponies are trotting or for one semester each academic year.

Employment in our second life becomes another tool of opportunity. If we keep our skills sharp and current, our teeth in, and our antennae up to job availabilities, it allows us to afford to expand the number of things we can do with the earnings.

"Money is a kind of disease that those who have it don't like to spread."

Mendel Maranz

There are some tricks to happiness in post-retirement jobs, too. One is to pick a field you love, usually one you've explored on your own (or wanted to) while you were working. Hobbies or special skills are a place to start. Then thoroughly research the job market, and if you find something, go right for it. But if there's little available, become a volunteer in the field: they are the first to hear when spots open. Finally, just be yourself, buoying your maturity and experience with a youthful enthusiasm.

Our will

How we plan this life is directly influenced by which or how many of our goods we want to—or think we should—leave behind.

Are our kids dragging out their lives until they get our inheritance? Do they grow pale at the prospect of us finally visiting Greece "on their money"? Are they living in cardboard shacks until they get the plantation? Is there an "ex" waiting to sue for the booty? Should we think about getting a direct-feed resuscitator so no one can find the plug?

Or are we hoping to spend every last dime?

If it's the latter, then Stephen Pollan and Mark Levine's book, *Die Broke*, provides a step-by-step process so we can live this life fully while creating the needed security and income flow to make that happen.

Or we can take a modified road between leaving a bundle or nothing by cutting it as close as possible and leaving, by default, anything that's still unspent.

"Age is only a number, a cipher for the records. A man can't retire his experience. He must use it. Experience achieves more with less energy and time."

Bernard Baruch on his 85th birthday

The *Die Broke* approach has much to commend it for any Super Second Lifer, even if leaving an intended or accidental inheritance isn't important. It is based on four key points: (1) quit our job today, (2) pay almost everything with cash, using credit only in emergency and for things that are too expensive, like homes and cars, (3) don't retire, and (4) die broke.

Quitting our job today means quitting mentally. Forget corporate loyalty—the corporations have forgotten us. Don't use our jobs to define who we are. Simply sell our services to the highest bidder, then give that lucky boss the kind of work they are paying for. Become a free agent, and always keep our eyes open. Don't confuse emotional wealth with financial wealth; that is, don't expect the job to feed us emotionally. Look for that elsewhere. Then if the job does provide emotional support, all the better.

Paying cash makes us more aware of what we're spending by slowing the whole process down. We see the actual money leaving our hands. We write ourselves one check a week for all the expenses.

Don't retire—always keep working. We'll probably need the income, we'll stay better informed, and we'll have fresh money to finance our dreams. Say Pollan and Levine, "Look at your working life as a lifelong journey up and down hills rather than a single climb up a steep cliff that ends with a fatal step off the edge (and into the abyss) at the arbitrary age of sixty-five." The idea is as much to stay active as earning: going to school, working part-time, starting a business. But always earning or learning.

And die broke. They cite four reasons why it no longer makes sense to leave inheritances: (1) Creating and maintaining an estate does damage to the person doing the hoarding—the problem of whether to spend for yourself or leave it to the kids, (2) It hurts society; the frozen investments contribute little to the productivity of the economy, (3) It hurts families because the dynamics of the relationships suffer, and (4) It hurts the recipient. It erodes their motivation and drive to work.

If we want to share our wealth with our kids, or others, why let the state dilute it through taxation? Why not just give gifts (up to the $10,000 annual tax-free maximum) when they most need it and we can most afford it?

How would Pollan and Levine have us spend our money, after meeting obligations? On experiences and education.

Die Broke gives the details and the order, including excellent advice about annuities, reverse mortgages, various forms of insurance, and serial investing (for a home, college, then retirement).

Some additional, important thoughts

Let's share some particularly appropriate second life financial guidelines, plucked from the best current financial planning books, compressed into 26 action steps, and divided into two categories: (1) income and assets and (2) expenses.

These make particular sense if you have a financial feel for where you are now and a rough notion for where you might be at key stages in the future. You can get that by completing the worksheets a few pages back—or you may wish to use the tables in Daniel Kehrer's *Kiplinger's 12 Steps to a Worry-Free Retirement* (pages 20-3) or Ralph Warner's *Get a Life: You Don't Need a Million to Retire Well* (pages 170 and 200), both widely found in local libraries. See the source list at the end of this chapter.

Income and Assets

Want to know how much you will receive? Call (800) 772-1213

"Never invest your money on anything that eats or needs repainting."

Billy Rose

1. Plan on receiving Social Security (or the equivalent). As we said earlier, it may provide about 40% of our needs. Most seniors need from 60-75% of their pre-retirement income to live modestly in retirement. Figure 70%. Social Security will also continue to pay after we die, helping provide for our latter-life children (until 16, longer if in college), our spouse (even ex-spouses, sometimes), and dependent parents. Doomsayers notwithstanding, Social Security may look a bit different but it will still be around.

2. Most of the rest of our retirement income will probably come from our pension at work, similar programs if we are self-employed (like Keogh and SEP-IRAs), and from any IRA money we slipped out annually before filing taxes. If we lucked into some form of "golden parachute" for early retirement, that can be a big help too. For most, pensions and savings are what later provide that needed 30% of our present income for a more comfortable second life.

3. Add to that any additional savings or personal investments (like money market stocks, bonds, property, collectibles, or annuities) and we may already have more than we need to do as we wish later.

4. If we do, bingo—because the moment our second life starts that money isn't going to simply fall in our hands! We will extract it in planned portions, with the principal continuing to earn compound interest as long as it lasts, which may be long after we are using the bank eternal!

5. Not planing to retire? All the better. Any income we continue to earn once we are at the comfort stage keeps adding up and compiling more interest, which earns even more interest. We can even delay drawing Social Security for a

few more years, earning an additional 8%, inflation adjusted.

6. If our folks or kin were kind enough to leave us some form of inheritance, that could proportionally increase our financial freedom. (Alas, if that kind soul had gifted it instead during their life, they would have probably saved in taxes and we could have been investing that too, compounded, to free us up even more. But we don't want to sound ungrateful.)

7. Sometimes, sadly, somebody dies and we are the beneficiary of their life insurance. But we can't depend on this—and it's imprudent to speed it up. Still, it means more funds, which means more choices.

8. While not income per se, if we have insured ourselves for disability and that occurs, that may help keep us solvent in our later years.

9. And we will have access to Medicare and Medicaid (or whatever they are called) to help offset our main health costs. Like Social Security, some sort of net will be there.

10. Most people enter their second lives with a home mortgage substantially or totally paid. (The happiest retirees are those without house payments at all. Many of them got there—and saved as much as $150,000 or more in interest—by fattening up their monthly mortgage payments. They probably paid their credit cards first, then slipped in a few extra bucks on the mortgage principal each time.) If we subtract the house payments, we also need less income. And kids gone can reduce our annual expenses as much as $15,000 each.

11. Having a low or paid mortgage can be a financial boon if we down-scale and sell the big house, which is easier to do if the kids are gone and we tell freeloaders that we have become deranged. Or we can simply live there forever and either will it to our heir(s), Pollan and Levine be damned, or we can use it as a new source of steady income through reverse mortgaging, should our health or other expenses outpace our savings—or we live far too long!

"Life insurance is like a parachute. If you ever need it and haven't got it, you will never need it again."

12. Another way to "find" income is to take any savings we make by not having to pay credit card interest or not having car payments and put that amount either into the bank to compound or to add it to the mortgage payment. When we make the last house payment, we might take a victory trip on what we would have had to pay the next month or two, then put the subsequent monthly non-payments into our own account. Since we're used to spending that money anyway, why not give it to ourselves to grow on our own behalf?

13. When we sell off the toys—the boat, the snowmobile, the trailer, etc.—we not only get a boost in bucks, we no longer have to pay for their upkeep, license, or storage.

14. There's another win-win that, if done right, can bring as much joy as income: if single, marry again, pool your combined retirement holdings, and cuddle into the twilight! Prenuptial agreements are in order here, even if we're Willard Scott regulars in the centenary club.

Expenses

15. The main idea in our second life is to not let our expenses get ahead of our budgeted reserves and income.

16. But life isn't always that kind; the two are seldom in perfect balance. We can't just keep making soup of our pets or lowering the winter heat. When or if it gets out of balance, we must get some advice, cut back on the excessive spending, or find some new income, like reverse mortgaging or taking on a part-time job.

17. While we won't spend nearly as much in retirement as we did before (unless we go batty), we will continue to have bills that must be paid: maybe a house payment or rent, utilities, phone, doctor, and food. Those are the core costs that our savings should meet.

18. Physical and mental health are more important than money, it's said, so if we are blessed with good health, we should spend to keep it so. If not, we must get it as good as possible, then sustain or improve it. That means that the costs for treatment, medicine, fitness or exercise, transportation, education, and some entertainment have high priority. Also long-term insurance, which should be considered and probably begun when we are young and healthy.

"The reason many people don't live within their incomes is that they don't consider that living."

19. The happiest retirees are the most active, so other elements of that high quality of life might be travel, hobbies, public service, even pets. Volunteering and personal growth aren't free either, but those expenditures can be especially valuable.

20. The biggest fear of most retirees is that the moment they leave a secure job they will catch or suffer some disastrous malady and be consigned to a full-care facility for their last 30 years! A foolish fear, numbers tell us, since the percentage of people in a nursing home at any one time is 5.2%. (Most of those spend less than a year there, often their last.) So the million-dollar reserve nest egg for that "certainty" probably costs ten times its worth in ulcers, overtime, and exhausted spouses during our prime earning years.

21. But we will have health costs, so an important budget item is insurance, then Medicare supplements, and finally personal money for co-payments, full payments, and prescriptions. This usually stabilizes and the cost is manageable. Often it goes down in the final years.

22. One expense that can put a big dent in our budget is a car. If we're used to buying a new car every 40 minutes (worse yet, leasing one), we must think twice or thrice. It's best to wait to buy until we have the cash, or get a car that's a year or two older, or keep our current clunker rolling.

23. Divorce is a real second life bummer. It can reduce a well-financed couple to two marginal survivors. One solution? Strengthen the marriage earlier so at retirement it is intact. One way to do that is to actively collaborate to make Super Second Lives a dual reality.

24. If we're still using credit cards with abandon, we've simply got to get our expenses on a tighter budget. Unless our cards have no or a low fee, the 18-24% interest can quickly undermine years of sensible saving. Reduce the cards to one, then limit its use to emergencies or for big-ticket items.

25. We may still have lingering obligations into our retirement years, like assumed debts for our kids' schooling. It's best to pay them off as soon as possible, to lower our monthly outflow.

26. The hardest financial burden is when we are entering our own second lives with dependent parents, bless them. But it may not be nearly as bad as it appears. We must sit down and figure out their income or support sources—like pensions, savings, and Medicare—before assuming that their entire support will all have to come from our savings.

This information should help us better prep for a freer future. But what do we do with the four model worksheets?

We will need at least the Money Worksheet for Chapter 13, "Financial Resources Must Now be Added to the Action Plan," and Chapter 14, "The Final Action Plan." The Net Worth Worksheet tells both where we are now and where we will be financially.

We can create a worksheet for each year or for coming time-pegs, usually at the start or end of five- or ten-year time periods based on age, i.e., 60. While the basic income and expenditures may vary some annually, the key item is (E), the maximum income deficit or surplus. If a surplus, that's what we have to finance our dreams. If a deficit, attention may be needed to keep the ship afloat!

Financial or Investment Sources

Gerber, Michael E., ***The E-Myth Revisited***. (Harper Business, 1995). If you're going to start a business, this is *must* reading.

Godin, Seith, ***If You're Clueless about Retirement Planning and Want to Know More***. (Dearborn, 1997).

Holzer, Bambi, ***Retire Rich: The Baby Boomer's Guide to a Secure Future***. (Wiley, 1998).

Keefe, Carol, ***How to Get What You Want in Life With the Money You Already Have***. (Little, Brown, 1995).

Kehrer, Daniel, ***Kiplinger's 12 Steps to a Worry-Free Retirement***, 2nd ed., revised and updated (Random House, 1995). Has excellent charts to see where you are and what you need, though the figures are getting dated and you'd have to save millions, using their formula, to retire worry-free.

Keithley, M.C., ***Retire Early Retire Well***. (Invesmart Publications, 1997).

Parrott, William W. and John L. Parrott, ***You Can Afford to Retire! A No-Nonsense Guide to Pre-Retirement Financial Planning*** (N.Y. Institute of Finance, 1992). Also dated.

Patterson, Martha Priddy, ***The Working Woman's Guide to Retirement Planning: Saving and Investing Now for a Secure Future***. (Prentice Hall, 1993). Getting dated.

Petras, Kathryn and Ross, ***The Only Retirement Guide You'll Ever Need.*** (Poseidon Press, 1991). Not exactly, but it does cover a lot of ground.

Pollan, Stephen and Mark Levine, ***Die Broke.*** (HarperBusiness, 1997). Clear, usable process that shows how to spend and give all your money in this life. Other practical advice for second lifers too.

Scholen, Ken, ***Your New Retirement Nest Egg: A Consumer Guide to New Reverse Mortgages.*** (NCHEC Press, 1995). Last resort financing, but an excellent guide.

Wall, Ginita and Victoria F. Collins, ***Your Next Fifty Years: A Completely New Way to Look at How, When, and If You Should Retire.*** (Henry Holt, 1998). Retire? they ask. Solid, straightforward thinking.

Warner, Ralph, ***Get a Life: You Don't Need a Million to Retire Well.*** (Nolo Press, 1996). Realistic, easy to read with interesting interviews with second lifers. Promises you won't end up a bag person, unless of course bags are your thing.

For a list of aging-related financial or investment organizations (with address, phone, and website), please see the Appendix.

Part Two

Planning, Implementing, and Living Your
Super Second Life

A Super Second Life Dream List Comes First...

8

It starts with a seemingly simple question, "If you had all the money, time, and energy you needed and were free from any outside constraints, what would you do in your extra 30 years?"

That's the first step to creating your Super Second Life, to opening the gates to every future avenue you may wish to enjoy.

The idea is to put on paper anything that comes to mind, however bizarre, rational, flighty, heart-pounding, mundane, spine-tingling, impractical, thought-provoking, or ephemeral.

To help, this chapter provides the reason, the tools, and the form needed to create your own dream list while it also begins a parallel feature: an example that helps guide you through the steps suggested in the chapters that follow.

Do you have a mate or playmate you want to spend those future years with? No problem. It also has an example and instructions for that too: how to both blend and bend your future lives to accommodate each of your needs.

It starts with a dream. This chapter elicits dreams.

Creating your own world

To have a super real world is to realize your dreams.

So to initiate, then define your Super Second Life, you must first project yourself beyond your daily activities, uncertainty, aging, and doubt. You must dream.

You must ask yourself, "If I could control every aspect of my life, how would I want to live my remaining days? What would that look like? What would be the touchstones of that existence?"

Mind pictures. Word pictures. A created view. Dreams.

You and I know that these are dreams. That we can't control many, certainly not all aspects of our lives.

But we must dream anyway. Without the vision, nothing happens. Our next life becomes an extension of this life, with wrinkles. We might make changes but they will be done without a grander design.

Think of our Super Second Life as changing our life abode, or creating a new home for our activities in the next 30 or so years. Would we simply pile sticks and shingles on our present place, without regard to why we need a new house, how it might best serve us, and what it must do to protect us properly?

Doesn't it make a lot more sense to first figure out where we want this new, final house to be located? Then what we plan to do in this house, so we know the number and kind of rooms, its height and design, and what needs it must meet? Wouldn't we then create a detailed blueprint so it could be built quickly, strongly, and as we wish?

A lot of dreaming is needed for that blueprint.

As a lot of dreaming is required for a Super Second Life, which will be your physical, emotional, and spiritual home for the rest of your days.

You must make your dreams come true

Dr. Michael Gerber says it best in **The E-Myth Revisited** when he describes Your Primary Aim as "the story of your life, the script you create now. First you must write it. Then you must make it come true."

It's no different for the second half of your life. It may be even more important because by then you have the wisdom, skills, and money to truly enact that script.

Everybody lives but it takes greatness to elevate yourself by your own intentions.

Again, Gerber hits the target:

Great people have a vision of their lives that they practice emulating each and every day... The difference between great people and everyone else is that great people create their lives actively, while everyone else is created by their lives, passively waiting to see where life takes them next. The difference between the two is the difference between living fully and just existing. The difference between the two is living intentionally and living by accident.

In our context, Second Life greatness starts with dreams. Ask yourself what seems to be a simple question, "If you had all the money, time, and energy you needed and were free from any outside constraints, what would you do in your extra 30 years?"

None of the four is likely to be completely unrestricted, of course—some will surely pinch tighter than others—but asking anything less reduces your dream flow.

Brainstorming

This is how a Super Second Life begins, by asking this broad, tough question to elicit every conceivable answer, to open the gate to every future avenue.

The idea is to put on paper anything that comes to mind, however bizarre, rational, flighty, heart-pounding, mundane, spine-tingling, impractical, thought-provoking, or ephemeral.

Create an open-ended list, to be added to in the days, weeks, and years to follow. Don't edit. Don't judge. Just write.

This creates a starting post for each point made, so it can be explored as fully as possible, to identify all the related points, thoughts, and dreams they prompt, all to help further define concrete, realizable goals for a Super Second Life.

"Middle age is when you have met so many people that every new person you meet reminds you of someone else and usually is."

Ogden Nash

You're not starting with a blank page or a *tabula rasa*—if you completed the "Me Now" lists in Chapter 2 and the "In" and "Out" Lists in Chapter 4. You are aware of general things you like about yourself and some areas you want to explore to greater depth.

You also know what you don't like, or what doesn't work for you.

A pair of other, very general guidelines will provide some additional guidance. You now have an overview of your health, which may suggest some physical or emotional boundaries. And you know on which deck of the ship you will see the sea from your various financial worksheets. Or if you'll be rowing or wading! Starter toeholds that will keep your dreams within the reach of reality.

Keeping track

How do keep track of these dreams?

For starters, all you need is paper, a pencil, and some distance—from distractions that interrupt your dreaming.

Write down everything that comes up. Don't worry about spelling, grammar, context, or even sense. Some ideas will pop out somewhere along their path of development, like a tree first suggesting itself as bark or a leaf or even its own shadow. Capture everything on paper, and if it's bewildering now, let it grow or rest until it later suggests a better word or vision.

Then capture those dreams in a word or phrase and write them in the Super Second Life Dream List, which is the starting point for a later Action Plan.

At this point, don't belabor the details. It's unimportant whether you want to do whatever is listed now, in five years, or as a farewell. Don't worry about its cost or even its practicality. Erase mentally the dozens of reasons why it may be difficult or nearly impossible. Err on the side of including far too many dreams. Write pages and pages of your latter-day wish list.

I wouldn't share it with family or friends yet. It needs more work. We will refine these ideas and prioritize them later.

Some will prove unworkable; some will disappear, to re-emerge in a different form; some will germinate and produce a half-dozen related dreams. You're really planting an idea garden. Make your mind fertile. Plant any dream that emerges. Later we'll see which of them grow.

Here's the form. Why not make a copy and get started planning your future?

SUPER SECOND LIFE DREAM LIST

NAME _____ Date _____

DREAMS
1.
2.
3.
4.
5.
6.
7.
8.
9.
10.
11.
12.
13.
14.
15.
16.
17.
18.
19.
20.
21.
22.
23.
24.
25.
26.
27.
28.

If this is a library book or is available for multiple or public use, do <u>not</u> write on this form.
Please copy this or the example in the Appendix, then write on your copy. Thank you.

Creating your own
Super Second Life
Dream List

Did you write some down? Did you run out of dreams? Remember to simply list what you want to do in the future. Then add and adjust, and delete, as the future arrives.

Form a mental picture of yourself as you'd like to be at some point in the future, then break that down into steps to make your larger dreams and wishes come true.

Starter questions for your mental picture might be:

1. How do you see yourself, ideally, at 60, 70, 80, ...?
2. Are you married, single, with a companion?
3. Are you still involved vocationally or professionally?
4. What is your financial state? How is your health?
5. Describe your relationships. Family ties? Friends?
6. What hobbies or activities are you enjoying?
7. What's important to you?
8. Are you spiritually active?
9. Any burial or death wishes?

Now, translate your picture views into specifics. For example, to #8, "Are you spiritually active?", you might put into sentence form what you would do to make your answer become a future reality, such as

1. Become a church deacon.
2. Visit the Holy Wall (Mother Church, Vatican, etc.)
3. Pray daily.
4. Actively support the orphanage in _____, Guatemala.

Don't worry about chronology—the order of future events or activities. Later you will time-peg the list, placing your dreams into approximate time frames. Just get the future plans or ideas down now.

What others
dream of doing

Let me share some solid examples from participants in my "Creating Your Own Super Second Life" workshop to give you a starter idea of what you might put on your list. Of course, you need you own dreams. Like wigs and prom dresses, they work best form-fit!

A COMPOSITE, BORROWED DREAM LIST

conquer my fear of flying
overcome general fears
get a part-time winery job
set up wise investment plan
take a trip without a destination
begin volunteer work with teens
change my profession
get an MFCC license
travel to New Orleans
travel to Ireland
travel to India, see Himalayas
travel to Northern Italy
improve my photography skills
write travel articles
spend more time with friends
   and family
exercise
shape up my kids

donate more time to charities
research my family tree
learn French
volunteer with Habitat for
   Humanity
create circle of supportive
   friends
live in South America
live in Italy
reduce my credit cards to one
achieve emotional balance
go to Europe on the QE2
buy a house
expand my real estate consulting
   business
become a dog custodian
certify as a water aerobics
   instructor
deepen my spiritual life

(For 200 more ideas, see the Appendix.)

An example

It's one thing for me to tell you to plan your extra 30 years. It's another thing for me to do it myself—publicly!

Alas, what follows is an example of *my* Action Plan and quest for a Super Second Life.

While I'm not eager to display my last wart and vain whim in print with all of America (and maybe even Canada), the biggest problem is that I'm not an ideal 40-55, but just 61 as this book is being written. Thus I already have a 6D shoe firmly planted in my own Super Second Life—audaciously, since both of my grandfathers rushed to the hereafter at 56! Which means that I'm actually doing some of the things now that I also want to do later.

Would you like to see the Super Second Life plans of five other people who have different dreams and means?

Since this chapter asks for dreams (or plans) for a Super Second Life Dream List, I repaired for two hours to Waller Park in Santa Maria, California, one warm, breezy afternoon and filled out two pages of the personal "dreams" that follow. I'm certain that in the coming days, and months, since I've put

Me too! If you are reading this book and would like to share your plans with others, please e-mail me at **gb@agemasters.com** *and I will explain what is needed to make that happen.*

I will then post five other examples at a time, and change them when appropriate, at the website: **www.agemasters.com.**

These should appear in October, 1999.

my creative juices flowing that direction, there will be more to add. So I reserve the right (as I advise you to do) to personally modify the list as I see fit, actually until the day I die. (I can hear the ghosts of my grandfathers chuckling and checking their big pocket watches.)

As suggested earlier, I found it easier to begin with some picture views of how I would like to see myself at some point in my discerning, 55+ years—say, at 65 or 70—and again, later, then break those down into the specifics listed below.

For the discerning years, I would like to see myself this way: happily married, actively speaking, well informed both generally and about my professional fields, well traveled, living within my financial means so I can stay independent, purposely exercising and staying healthy, musically active and growing, expanding my computer graphics knowledge, staying in touch through a website, well rounded socially, maintaining and gathering new friends, and closely tied to my and my wife's families.

I added more hopes too, for those later, reflective years when independence is less likely: to remain active, reading, seeking community, and in touch with my family. I don't want to be kept alive by artificial means nor do I want my death to be a financial burden to others. Finally, to pass with dignity and to donate my organs and body for use by others.

Adapted from those global hopes, this is what my dream list looks like:

SAMPLE SUPER SECOND LIFE DREAM LIST

NAME: Gordon Burgett

DREAMS
1. Remain happily married for our lives.
2. Sell my D.C.U. / M.C.U. publishing firm.
3. Phase out my C.U. publishing firm, probably between ages 65-70.
4. Offer 25-50 seminars annually at the California university/college level for about two more years.

5. Speak to associations, corporations, other groups about Super Second Life, 2-3 times a month until about 68 (or when it isn't fun).
6. Write a new book every two years, until about 68; including Perfect Human World book.
7. Include in the new books a novel or two.
8. Learn to play the piano with both hands.
9. Buy (or rent) a cello and learn to play that too.
10. Have 1.5-2 hours a day for uninterrupted reading.
11. Play 18 holes of golf weekly with three other cronies.
12. Play a practice nine holes of golf weekly, alone or with selected friends.
13. Take one half- or full-day nature hike a month; a couple a year overnighters.
14. Travel annually to see my brothers, alternating them each year.
15. Travel to visit my wife's folks and family once a year.
16. Travel abroad for two weeks every 18 months or so; targets: Australia/New Zealand, Brazil, Ireland, Europe. Particularly walking trips in Ireland, Wales, England.
17. See a minimum of two live plays or concerts a month.
18. Increase my activity with the local Barbershopper's group: weekly practice, perform with them when possible, attend a convention annually, later join a quartet.
19. Continue a steady exercise regimen at the local YMCA: run, cycle, or swim each once or twice a week (plus ab exercises, jacuzzi, and steam room after each session).
20. Continue my Agemasters achievements as long as possible: cycle my age in miles (then kms); attempt to swim my age in kms; run my age at 62 in kms; add in walking my age later.
21. Learn more about computer graphic design: classes, upgrade computer and software.
22. Maintain an active website.
23. Attend movies regularly with wife and friends.
24. Visit my daughters and their families regularly (at least quarterly).
25. Maintain close contact with my wife's daughters and families.
26. Create or expand a Burgett genealogical family tree.
27. Maintain close contact with my sister and family.
28. Remain active in professional publishing, speaking, and writing associations or affiliations as long as it is appropriate. Continue contributing through their web activities.
29. Continue the Pathfinders consulting program.
30. Perform in the *Messiah* 1-3 times annually in Holiday Season.
31. In health, keep my weight at 150-8, continue taking thyroid and allergy medications.
32. Financially, maintain regular control over finances.
33. Find a sponsor / buyer for my Agemasters Athletic Recognition program; serve as spokesman and on the Board of Directors, if possible.
34. After travel has ended, adopt an older pet.
35. Check into Elderhostel program for combination education/travel programs.
36. Check into AmeriCorps Senior Corps programs; see if consulting in writing fits in.
37. Look into creating oral histories, for Burgett archives; help city and/or other groups conduct the interviews for their programs.

If you have a spouse or partner?

Congratulations! They are people too, entitled to their own hopes and dreams. They also need to create their own dream lists, and later Action Plans.

Why? Because you may not reach old age and they will have to fend, and grow, without you, hard as that may be to imagine. Or you may not reach old age mated. Or you may find yourselves still mated but drifting into separate orbs of action. So everybody should know what they want to do with their own extra 30 years...

In that enlightened spirit, I asked my wife to create her own list, without consulting mine first. (She is a decade younger than I and, at 50, plunk in the ideal 40-55 year old initial planning period.) You'll see that in a second.

What will we do with our lists? Later we will compare them, and perhaps add or subtract a bit from our own lists, influenced by the new ideas the mate proposed. Then we will time-peg them, to see what is planned for when. Finally, we will divide the two lists into (1) a co-funded budget sheet and (2) a personal budget sheet.

More on that later. For now, here is my wife's Dream List:

SUPER SECOND LIFE DREAM LIST

NAME: Marsha Freeman Burgett

DREAMS
1. Have a warm, supportive, loving marriage.
2. Sell the publishing company.
3. Join forces with a leading consulting firm to sopify the dental world.
4. Give 60 speaking presentations in the next 12 months, 90 the following.
5. Retire from consulting and speaking at 60.
6. Maintain $500,000 in some form of savings, retirement funds, or investment accounts.
7. Maintain my weight at 125-130 pounds.
8. Be physically active through golf, walking, cycling, calisthenics, and sports.
9. Visit my family in Tulsa and Arkansas four times a year.
10. Visit my husband's daughters and family four times a year.
11. Create a family album, with notes explaining the photos.

12. Own a comfortable home that is a haven from the outside world.
13. Interact with my children/grandchildren three to four times a week.
14. Live a life of simplicity: keep what I use and treasure and give the rest away.
15. Surround myself with warm, supportive, creative, positive-minded people.
16. Go to mass weekly and pray daily.
17. Read a book a week: per month, one biography, two novels, and one business or self-help book.
18. Listen to one motivational tape a week.
19. Read the daily paper and weekly/monthly periodicals.
20. Travel overseas every year or two: goals are Australia, England, Germany, Austria. Egypt, France, Ireland.
21. Meet Madeleine Albright.
22. See all of the NBA teams play.
23. Become a volunteer for Special Olympics, learn-to-read programs, and/or women's issues.
24. Complete a doctorate in psychology.
25. Become a licensed MFCC.
26. Create a college trust fund for my grandchildren.
27. Buy a powerful laptop computer that will allow me to quickly access the Internet and to e-mail family and friends.
28. Have a positive impact on everyone I meet.
29. Become financially secure, wise, and responsible.
30. Enjoy plants, particularly flowers.
31. Go on an annual retreat with women friends.
32. Send cards and notes for all birthdays and special events.
33. Mentor others.
34. Learn Spanish.
35. Write a how-to standard operating procedures book for the masses.
36. Entertain friends monthly.
37. Sightsee: visit historical sites, museums, art galleries, natural wonders.
38. Sew for pleasure.
39. Teach or counsel after I retire from working in the field of dentistry.
40. Be brave, courageous, disciplined, principled, and ethical, and live a life of integrity and honesty.
41. Watch the history channel at least once a week.

Enough dawdling. Fill in Your Super Second Life Dream List!

"For most men there should come a time of shifting harness, of lightening the load one way and adjusting it for greater effectiveness in another. That is the time for the second career, time for the old dog to perform new tricks. The new career may bring in little money; it may be concerned only with good works. On the other hand, it may bring in much needed support. It can be a delight to a man who comes at last to a well-earned job instead of a well-earned rest.

Dr. Wilder Penfield

Dreams Sometimes Have a Built-in Clock...

9

Not every dream works at every age. Few soccer stars began at 80.

The best way to form fit your future is to match your dreams to the time periods when they might work best. So this chapter shows how that is done, with four time boxes as starters into which you can guesstimate your dreams with your likely future capacity and desires. They are called time-pegs.

Still getting a lift from kite-flying at 70, though it was slotted for 60-69? Forget the slot and keep soaring! Turning 77 and you can't imagine why you planned to plant a rhubarb orchard now—or ever? Forget about it and do something more fun.

Time pegging simply gives temporal order to your future life.

It also lets you see where you might get a kick start when you are 40-55, so you've got the instructional or experiential background to excel later.

Every dream has its hour. Here you time-peg your future schedule.

Most dreams are age-appropriate

Look closely at that barnyard of Super Second Life dreams you've rounded up and penned on paper. Strange how unlike many of them are. They have different ages too.

That is, some are appropriate for mid-summer chickens, others just fine for last-leg roosters.

107

For example, if scaling the ten tallest Rockies is your wildest second life dream, great! But good luck if you're 97 and grappling with 400-400 vision! Mountain climbing is an early-bird dream, when (if ever) you have the strength, legs, desire, and deep-reach reserve.

Yet reading to your grandchildren (or children or great-great grandchildren) is a delight at any time. And if you weren't blessed with grandchildren, there are millions of somebody else's who would love to sit on your lap or at your feet to hear about *The Little Engine That Could* or *Green Eggs and Ham*.

What this chapter asks is that you take your dreams and time-peg them by putting them into broad time brackets so you can realize them at your best moments.

Time-peg them

Among the four saddest words in any language are "if I had only..." While you may, in fact, not realize all of the dreams you list, it's fairly certain that without time-pegging them, one or many will simply fall by the doable wayside. (Some may anyway, but not for wont of planning...)

An example comes immediately to mind.

I climbed to the top of Half Dome, in California's breathtaking Yosemite Park, when I was 57 with my younger daughter. The 17-mile, 4900-foot climb literally lasted from dawn to dusk. We had discussed it for nearly a year, so we dressed appropriately, brought plenty of water, and pursued the climb so we could spend enough time at the top to thoroughly absorb the spectacular view.

"Life consists not in holding good cards but in playing those you do hold well."

Josh Billings

Kim was in her 20s then so she still had 35+ years to repeat the venture. But I didn't, and as I write this book I'm fully aware that my vertical hiking days are drawing to a close. I think I could do it again right now, and I suspect that until about 65 I'll be up to the rigors. But after that I'm not sure I'd want to even if I could.

The lesson is clear: put your dreams that have temporal limits in an achievable order, and let the others without time restraints fall whenever they comfortably fit.

How many brackets you create is up to you. Some prefer three time-pegs: (1) the "middle years," from 40-55, to get the most vigorous activities under their belt; (2) the "discerning years," for about 20 years after 55, and (3) the "reflective years," from about 75 and up.

A case can also be made for four or five: (1) from 40-55, (2) 55-65, (3) 65-75, (4) 75-85 or so, and (5) thereafter.

Another, far less precise way is to simply take your dreams and stack them up by the order you think you can do them, the most urgent or compelling on top. Then if one or the other seems beyond the pale when its turn comes, you either scale it down to make it doable or you throw it out, with a shrug and a laugh.

The purpose of this book is not to regiment older age or to herd dreams into concrete corrals but simply to put realizable goals in convenient time spots, much like you put implements in the rooms where they are most used and enjoyed. There's little as irksome as a bench tool that is suddenly residing in the attic or a pot holder, when immediately needed, that wended its way to somebody's bedroom.

So time-pegging dreams is your task, if you wish.

Incidentally, some of this is already done, in a very general way. If you used a "Picture Plan" to envision how you would see yourself at various times, that can be translated quickly into a respective time-peg.

In my case, my examples were broken into discerning and reflective years, so the latter would fit into my last category. But since I'm now 61, there was no reason to consider a "middle year" category, when I would get a head start on my Super Second Years.

For your purposes, let me strike a compromise. I'll include four time boxes, or time-pegs, with approximate numbers that you simply replace with your own. Then I'll try to drive my own Dream List into these arbitrary holding pens.

"Who knows whether in retirement I shall be tempted to the last infirmity of mundane minds, which is to write a book."

Geoffrey Fisher, Archbishop of Canterbury

What Are You Going to Do With Your Extra 30 Years?

TIME-PEG #1—MIDDLE YEARS (40-55) / Date:
1.
2.
3.
4.
5.
6.
7.
8.
9.
10.

TIME-PEG #2—EARLY DISCERNING YEARS (55-68) / Date:
1.
2.
3.
4.
5.
6.
7.
8.
9.
10.

TIME-PEG #3—LATER DISCERNING YEARS (69-80) / Date:
1.
2.
3.
4.
5.
6.
7.
8.
9.
10.

TIME-PEG #4—REFLECTIVE YEARS (81+) / Date:
1.
2.
3.
4.
5.
6.
7.
8.
9.
10.

To time-peg my list I will have to change the boxes, given my current dotage. Let me use three of them and break them into decades: (1) 60-70, (2) 70-80, (3) 81+. (Since both of my grandmothers lived into their early 90s—more than 35 years longer than their mates—I'm eager to see how long I linger in #3!)

Here's how I see my list time-pegged. You will notice that some activities appear in two or three boxes, since those dreams are continual. Most also change in description as I grow older.

TIME-PEG #1— (60-70) / Date: xxx

1. Remain happily married for our lives.
2. Sell my D.C.U. / M.C.U. publishing firm.
3. Phase out my C.U. publishing firm, probably between ages 65-70.
4. Offer 25-50 seminars annually at the California university/college level, until about 62-3.
5. Speak to associations, corporations, other groups about Super Second Life, 2-3 times a month until about 68 (or it isn't fun).
6. Write a new book every two years, until about 68; including Perfect Human World book.
7. Include in the new books a novel or two.
8. Learn to play the piano with both hands.
9. Buy (or rent) a cello and learn to play that too.
10. Have 1.5-2 hours a day for uninterrupted reading.
11. Play 18 holes of golf weekly with three other cronies.
12. Play a practice nine holes of golf weekly, alone or with selected friends.
13. Take one half- or full-day nature hike a month; a couple a year overnighters.
14. Travel annually to see my brothers, alternating them each year.
15. Travel to visit my wife's folks and family once a year, at least as long as her folks live.
16. Travel abroad for two weeks every 18 months or so; targets: Australia/New Zealand, Brazil, Ireland, Europe. Particularly walking trips in Ireland, Wales, England.
17. See a minimum of two live plays or concerts a month.
18. Increase my activity with the local Barbershopper's group: weekly practice, perform with them when possible, attend a convention annually, later join a quartet.
19. Continue a steady exercise regimen at the local YMCA: run, cycle, or swim each once or twice a week (plus ab exercises, jacuzzi, and steam room after each session).
20. Continue my Agemasters achievements as long as possible: cycle my age in miles (then kms); attempt to swim my age in kms; at 62 run my age in kms; walk my age later.
21. Learn more about computer graphic design: classes, upgrade computer and software.
22. Maintain an active website.
23. Attend movies regularly with wife and friends.
24. Visit my daughters and their families regularly (at least quarterly).
25. Maintain close contact with my wife's daughters and families.
26. Create or expand a Burgett genealogical family tree.
27. Maintain close contact with my sister and family.
28. Remain active in professional publishing, speaking, and writing associations or affiliations as long as it is appropriate. Continue contributing through their web activities.
29. Continue the Pathfinders consulting program.
30. Perform in the *Messiah* 1-3 times annually in Holiday Season.
31. In health, keep my weight at 150-8, continue taking thyroid and allergy medications.
32. Financially, maintain regular control over finances.

33. Find a sponsor / buyer for my Agemasters Athletic Recognition program; serve as spokesman and on the Board of Directors, if possible.

34. Write a will, define my burial plans in writing, and finish steps to create a living trust.

35. Check into Elderhostel program for combination education/travel programs.

36. Check into AmeriCorps Senior Corps programs; see if consulting in writing fits in.

37. Look into creating oral histories, for Burgett archives; help city, other group conduct the interviews for their programs.

TIME-PEG #2 (70-80) / Date: xxx

1. Remain happily married for our lives.

2. Speak to associations, corporations, other groups about Super Second Life, 1-2 times a month as long as it is fun and I can maintain a high level of presentation.

3. Perhaps write novels, if successful earlier.

4. Play the piano (and cello).

5. Have 2 hours a day for uninterrupted reading.

6. Play 9-18 holes of golf weekly with three other cronies.

7. Practice nine holes of golf when I feel like it, alone or with selected friends.

8. Take one half-day nature hike a month.

9. Travel every year or two to see my brothers, alternating them.

10. Travel to visit my wife's folks and family, if her folks are still living.

11. Travel abroad occasionally.

12. Continue to see a one or two live plays or concerts a month.

13. If my voice and hearing are still acceptable, continue my activity with the local Barbershopper's group: weekly practice, perform with them when possible, attend a convention annually.

14. Continue a steady exercise regimen at the local YMCA.

15. If I'm still physically able, continue my Agemasters achievements at kilometer distances, particularly in cycling and walking.

16. Continue to expand and use my computer knowledge.

17. Maintain an active website.

18. Attend movies regularly with wife and friends.

19. Visit my daughters and their families regularly.

20. Maintain close contact with my wife's daughters and families.

21. Try not to fall off the living Burgett genealogical tree!

22. Maintain close contact with my sister and family.

23. Maintain friendships with those I knew in academia, speaking, and writing.

24. Perform in the *Messiah* annually during the Holiday Season, if the voice is satisfactory.

25. In health, keep my body and mind sound and as robust as possible.

26. Financially, maintain regular control over finances.

27. Adopt an older pet.

28. Participate in the Elderhostel program for combination education/travel programs.

TIME-PEG #3 (81+)   /   Date: xxx

1. Remain happily married for our lives.
2. Perhaps write novels, if it is still enjoyable.
3. Have 2+ hours a day for uninterrupted reading, with an occasional snooze.
4. Play 9 holes of golf weekly with other cronies.
5. Take a nature hike regularly.
6. Visit regularly with my brothers.
7. Visit with my wife's family when possible.
8. Travel domestically occasionally.
9. Continue to see live plays or concerts and movies as long as it is doable and enjoyable.
10. Sing, if I can, with Barbershop colleagues.
11. If possible and enjoyable, maintain a regular exercise regimen.
12. Visit my daughters and their families regularly.
13. Maintain close contact with my sister and family.
14. Maintain friendships with those I knew in academia, speaking, and writing.
15. In health, keep my body and mind sound and as robust as possible.
16. Financially, maintain regular control over finances.
17. Adopt an older pet.
18. Participate in the Elderhostel program for combination education/travel programs.
19. Remind Marsha of my burial plans and location of trust information.

My missing "Middle Years" time-peg!

I naturally regret not having read this book when I was younger so I could have revved up a bit and expanded my interests more during the 40-55 period, to be ready to do additional things at 60, and later at 70 or 80.

In that sense, I took a well-trod path of men my age, many who are unprepared to retire, having vested a huge period of their time and energy into their vocation and relatively little into friendship-creating (outside the job) or exploring outside activities that would provide enjoyable post-job recreation. So when the job is over, they are lost.

To help prevent that, a "middle years" time-peg helps those who have identified their Super Second Life goals test or prepare for what they think they'd like to do in their later lives.

How many fathers envision being the Judge Landis of the local Little League when they reach 60 or 70, only to discover that it's unbearable or boring or completely inappropriate?

A season on the Board while they were in their 40s or 50s would have prepped them accordingly.

How many women fantasize a stint on the City Council or Board of Education, only to find that a lack of earlier experience or political training made those hopes impossible?

How many of either gender postpone a thorough health check-up and sensible exercise and diet until all are forced upon them?

Another reason for a "middle years" time-peg is to be able to program and prioritize activities with children as they reach later school, college, and adulthood, to be able to continue the activities, as they are or modified by the changing situations, as all age.

Does that sound vague?

Let me focus on my Dream List and work backward, creating a hypothetical (and very short) "middle years" list, to provide a few examples, which I will later expand upon.

HYPOTHETICAL TIME-PEG (40-55) / Date: xxx
1. Volunteer to read and tape material for the Braille Institute.
2. Take refresher courses and digs in archeology at the local community college
3. Create a permanent, rotating internship with a local community college in my publishing firm.
4. Restring my violin, begin a strict practicing regimen, and join a local orchestra.
5. Begin piano lessons.

What might have been...

While in my case, at 61, this is simply looking backward, for others reading this book and beginning their projections for their Super Second Lives much earlier, this is where you can ease in the preliminary steps that make a richer later life possible.

For example, since I've spoken publicly for several decades and have created more than 25 audio cassette series, it should have occurred to me to share some of those vocal skills to help others to whom the spoken media is life-sustaining. Had I begun that earlier, it would have become as much a part of my future routine as my physical activities, writing, and Barbershopping. (It's not the best example, however, since I can begin this at any age...)

The second item, dusting up on archeology and participating in digs when I was 40 or 50, would have been done with a secondary intent, that of getting my daughters interested, joining in, and creating a new activity for all of us to do together.

The third would simply have enriched the lives of others, me, and those employed in my small publishing firm: to have brought in a new intern every school year, a journalism or computer graphics student who would have helped us and would have received hands-on, practical real world vocational experience. Alas, since the firm is soon to be sold, that door is closed.

In my youth, I was a mediocre violinist. I have the instrument and remember the fingering and bowing, but I've let it slide. If I had simply restrung the fiddle and begun practicing with any discipline, two things would now appear on my 60+ time-pegs: orchestra practice and cello lessons!

The fifth simply means that had I known I would have lived so long and would have a piano at my disposal, I'd have taken piano lessons a long time ago. A perfect example of getting a head start on many years of joy by taking lessons or getting involved earlier, to get the rudiments mastered when the fingers and mind are nimblest.

The point: take your dreams and match them to the time period when they can best be realized. And if you're under 55, ask which of those future dreams could you get started on now, to reach proficiency when you'll have time to bring them to their fullest fruition. (Or which you might then eliminate from your future plans, having tried them now and found them less fun or interesting than you thought.)

Dreams Must be Further Defined by Commitment and Prioritization | 10

It's one thing to have a dream, another to so want that dream to come true that you will commit all of your energy and skill to make it happen. So every dream must be evaluated by how much you really do want it.

That is, when you have your dream list completed, then time-pegged, it is time to subject it to some form of no-nonsense prioritization.

In this chapter I suggest a five-step evaluation process, with only those dreams that satisfy the fifth-step criterion making your Action Plan. The rest can wait, fully defined and hoping they will rise in dedication to acquire that degree of no-holds-barred allegiance.

Weigh your commitment, then focus on those things you must do.

Some dreams are just dreams

Let me say it again: It's one thing to have a dream, another to so want that dream to come true that you will commit all of your energy and skill to make it happen.

Many future dreams have a "wow!" element to them. A "wouldn't that be great..." component. Somewhere between mild enthusiasm and the bonanza incredulity of winning the lottery. But not a lot of commitment. If they happened, wow! But not enough belief that they will, or real joy that they might, to muster up much hard work or close planning.

117

Other dreams are firmer. "My destiny" dreams fall in this category. They are the culmination of all you've read, done, or wanted. If achieved, they are your destiny realized.

So there are levels of dreams, and there are degrees of how hard we are willing to do whatever it takes, or anything, to convert them into full-fleshed reality.

Levels of Commitment

The question is how you measure commitment, particularly of something projected to a distant or even near future.

The percentage approach is one form of measurement, but suspect.

"I want you guys to play 100% today!" is the classic call to action—and every baseball coach's desire. 100% is clear enough, but what is 98%? Throwing not quite as hard? And 93%? Sliding straight in instead of hooking? Moving your hands an inch up the bat? What if you wanted to play 100% but your skills lifted you only to 84%? And what if you only cared 75% but, despite yourself, you rose to 93% in performance?

I think what you really need to make sense of a Super Second Life plan is a cluster of no-holds-barred convictions at the core of your everyday activities. A cluster that will be scattered through the years, like the key stepping stones in a garden full of beauty.

That's why I like Dr. Robert Wubbolding's definition of commitment from his *Evaluation: The Cornerstone in the Practice of Reality Therapy* (1990). He says there are five levels of commitment:

Level 1. I don't want to and you can't help me.
Level 2. I want the results but I don't want to put in the effort.
Level 3. I'll try. I might. I could.
Level 4. I'll do the best I can (with what I currently know).
Level 5. I'll do whatever it takes (including what I don't know).

We're interested in number five. How does is differ from the first four?

It's almost the reverse of the first, which is the two-year-old's way of saying "No!" Teens use it too, without the con-

"All life is an experiment. The more experiments you make, the better."

Ralph Waldo Emerson

frontational terminology. They just dig in and do nothing. So did the viceroys to the King of Spain's colonial commands. "*Obedezco pero no cumplo*," meaning "I obey but I don't comply." It's not the absence of a commitment, rather the resolve to achieve the reverse result: "I won't do it!" rather than "A team of horses (or horse traders) couldn't stop me from making this happen!"

> "Life is a series of frontispieces. The way to be satisfied is never to look back."
>
> *William Hazlitt*

My wife describes the second as fully appropriate to her exercise pledge. She would love to have the results—without the sweat! Like planning to become rich at 71 if some unknown relative leaves you a windfall in their will. Not much proaction there to plan around.

And the third—"I'll try. I might, I could"—is about as lukewarm as a commitment can be. About as resounding as "I think I'll do that someday." In other words, no commitment at all. If, by some miracle, it should get done, it is better relegated to that class of unexplainable events that just happen somehow. Too weak for our use here.

"I'll do the best I can..." is the most insidious. It sounds good but one's "very best" always falls short of fulfillment. What makes it dangerous is that it contains the winds of commitment, a breath of potential—but at heart it's just hot air.

Still, a pledge at the fourth level might someday find the wings to rise above that hot air, plus the backbone to become a number five. Fours should be written down and kept visible on the long shot that they will ultimately win true commitment.

Top commitment

The only one that really counts is #5. "I'll do whatever it takes (including what I don't know." If your pledge is true, that contains the fire that brings results.

Let's say it now and set it aside. You can have a ton of commitment, all the skill and money necessary, and every ingredient for success at hand, and still not make or have a dream come true. Some explanations are understandable: you died first, a tornado carried away your tools, the needed mate took a powder... Or there is no explanation. Despite the desire and the near doing, it just didn't happen.

119

But only in the fifth and highest category is that the rare exception and not the inevitable rule.

By isolating those fives and focusing your efforts on them will your Super Second Life Action Plan have legs and make real sense. Which is precisely the purpose of this chapter, to ask you now to sort through the 15, 30, 60 things you have lined up to put joy and direction in your coming years, to discover and highlight those that you want to do so much that "you will do whatever it takes!"

Then, to not lose sight of other future goals, bunch the rest as number fours. If they happen, with or without effort on your part, so much richer is your fabric. Some might even rise to a top commitment, particularly as the most important dreams become realities and you gain confidence in your own ability to help make that happen.

The key threads are the fives. Around them you will build a happy older age.

Grading your dreams

We don't need new lists or boxes to complete the initial prioritization, though we will have to relist once that is done.

Simply take the time-peg boxes from the last chapter, find a red or colored pen, and to the left of the number on the list place an "X " by all of the #5 commitments. It's as easy as asking the question, "Will I want this enough to do whatever it takes to make it happen?"

How many "Xs" should you have? What percentage should be so designated?

Only you and "The Shadow" know. If there is one overriding thing you *must* do during a certain time slot and it is all you wish to focus on, then you have a list of one at that time. Sometimes your list is already lean—you've been subconsciously plucking—so most of the items listed will be in the #5 category.

Then reshuffle the various time-peg boxes so the highest priority, #5 items are at the top of that box. Draw or print a heavy line under the #5s. Under it, list the rest of the dreams you'd like to have come true but not so much that you'd divert your attention and time from making the key items happen.

"One cannot control the length of his life, but he can have something to say about its width and depth."

The example again

Here comes the example again!

Which items or activities on my three lists have a top-priority; that is, "Will I want this enough to do whatever it takes to make it happen?"

TIME-PEG (1): 60-70 YEARS
Gordon Burgett

1. Remain happily married for our lives.

2. Sell the D.C.U. / M.C.U. publishing firm.

3. Phase out my C.U. publishing firm, probably between ages 65-70.

5. Speak to associations, corporations, other groups about Super Second Life, 2-3 times a month until about 68 (or it isn't fun).

6. Write a new book every two years, until about 68; including Perfect Human World book.

10. Have 1.5-2 hours a day for uninterrupted reading.

11. Play 18 holes of golf weekly with three other cronies.

14. Travel annually to see my brothers, alternating them each year.

17. See a minimum of two live plays or concerts a month.

18. Increase my activity with the local Barbershopper's group: weekly practice, perform with them when possible, attend a convention annually, later join a quartet.

19. Continue a steady exercise regimen at the local YMCA: run, cycle, or swim each once or twice a week (plus ab exercises, jacuzzi, and steam room after each session).

20. Continue my Agemasters achievements as long as possible: cycle my age in miles (then kms); attempt to swim my age in kms; at 62 run my age in kms; add in walking my age later.

23. Attend movies regularly with wife and friends.

24. Visit my daughters and their families regularly (at least quarterly).

25. Maintain close contact with my wife's daughters and families.

27. Maintain close contact with my sister and family.

30. Perform in the *Messiah* 1-3 times annually in Holiday Season.

32. Financially, maintain regular control over finances.

TIME-PEG (2): 70-80 YEARS
Gordon Burgett

1. Remain happily married for our lives.

2. Speak to associations, corporations, other groups about Super Second Life, 1-2 times a month as long as it is fun and I can maintain a high level of presentation.

3. Perhaps write novels, if successful earlier.

7. Practice nine holes of golf when I feel like it, alone or with selected friends.

9. Travel every year or two to see my brothers, alternating them.

12. Continue to see a one or two live plays or concerts a month.

13. If my voice and hearing are still acceptable, continue my activity with the local Barbershopper's group: weekly practice, perform with them when possible, attend a convention annually.
14. Continue a steady exercise regimen at the local YMCA.
15. If I'm still physically able, continue my Agemasters achievements at kilometer distances, particularly in cycling and walking.
18. Attend movies regularly with wife and friends.
19. Visit my daughters and their families regularly.
20. Maintain close contact with my wife's daughters and families.
22. Maintain close contact with my sister and family.
23. Maintain friendships with those I knew in academia, speaking, and writing.
26. Financially, maintain regular control over finances.

TIME-PEG (3): 81+ YEARS
Gordon Burgett
1. Remain happily married for our lives.
3. Have 2+ hours a day for uninterrupted reading.
9. Continue to see live plays or concerts and movies as long as it is doable and enjoyable.
10. Sing, if I can, with Barbershop colleagues.
11. If possible and enjoyable, maintain a regular exercise regimen.
12. Visit my daughters and their families regularly.
13. Maintain close contact with my sister and family.
14. Maintain friendships with those I knew in academia, speaking, and writing.

An explanation

"Most people say that as you get old, you have to give up things. I think you get old because you give up things."

Senator Theodore Francis Green at 87

Of the 37 activities (or dreams) originally listed for the 60-70 time bracket, 18 survived that criterion. That strikes me as a lot of things to pursue, but it may be so because I'm actively doing many of them as I create the time-pegs—rather than doing this at, say, 43, and projecting it to a time period that doesn't begin for a dozen years. It may also be that none of them are all-encompassing or so vital it overwhelms the rest.

In any sense, they are there because I see them as fun, fulfilling, challenging, and vital to my life growth and worth.

A few are appropriate to a person still employed: either leave the work force or, in my case, stop or phase out of my self-employment. Another may be unusual: increasing my speaking (a lovely form of employment). The rest are predictable, given sufficient funds not to have to toil daily. I'll concen-

trate on recreation, reading, travel, the arts, family, singing, and watching my money disappear.

Frankly, it's not an overly ambitious list when compared to friends who speak of starting new businesses, building a car from scratch, umpiring several sports, cycling the West, and so on. I envy them but have been blessed with an active, mobile life and now find my joys in different ways. It's my list; it comes from my heart. Yours too must reflect your dreams.

Nor, in reading it for the first time, is it a particularly giving list. Not much volunteering, teaching the downtrodden, or building homes for the poor. I will reflect on that and perhaps find an area to enrich my life more by helping others. That's the good thing: the list isn't engraved but open to modification at any time.

But there are a few ambitious parts on it. I just joined the Santa Maria SPEBSQSA group and have a lot of harmonizing and lyric learning yet to do to fully contribute. I'd like to run 62 kilometers when I'm 62, cycle my age for some years to come, and maybe even swim it (at a kilometer a day) some day. And a book every two years simply slows down a pace I've maintained for the past 16 years—but novels are an exciting, fun wrinkle.

You'll note that some more challenging items were downgraded to a #4 level, and thus will appear on my list below the line of total commitment. Things like overseas travel every 18 months, studying the piano and cello, working on a family tree, and learning more about my computer while maintaining a website. Which doesn't mean that I won't do any or all of them. It means that I couldn't honestly say when I was weighing commitment that they were absolute top priority. Who knows? They may become so later, and get written into my Action Plan. Or I may just do them anyway and add them *de facto* into my life's activities, in addition to the other goals on the Action Plan.

The second time-peg, from 70-80, shrunk to 15 of 28, all but two of them a reduced continuation of what I was doing from 60-70. One of them isn't explicit but I'd like to cycle 70 miles when I'm 70, and perhaps do 70 kilometers in another sport or two. And I inserted that I'd like to maintain friendships

You must be tiring of my example, particularly if you abhor self-employment, think speakers are knaves, and find my dreams duller than workboots.

So once more, let me repeat my request from Chapter 8, so you can also see the dreams and plans of five other readers:

123

Would you like to see the Super Second Life plans of five other people who have different dreams and means?

Me too! If you are reading this book and would like to share your plans with others, please e-mail me at **gb@agemasters.com** *and I will explain what is needed to make that happen.*

I will then post five other examples at a time, and change them when appropriate, at the website: **www.agemasters.com.**

These should appear by October, 1999.

with those I knew in academia, speaking, and writing. These are current friends to whom I will add old acquaintances I seek out or encounter through the decade.

The 81+, the list has shrunk more, perhaps appropriately, to eight key areas: marriage, reading, singing and the arts, exercise, family, and friends. This is simply the core. I may surprise myself and horrify the world by writing a comic opera, inventing a gas glue, or helping resolve the border conflict between Peru and Ecuador.

Which is to say that my current priorities may, and probably will, change. That we aren't bound to our lists. They are, remember, simply favorite or desired stepping stones that we are mapping. We can redraw the map or add (or remove) the stones. That's the fun of playing with dreams.

A last thought. I apologize for using me as the example and dwelling too long on my own thoughts and goals. I could have invented a strawperson, but it strikes me as too artificial to make sense. Rather an imperfect author than a perfect dummy.

It's perhaps more important that I remind you that the example is being offered to help you take your steps to create your own Super Second Life. I learn by watching what others do, then applying that to my skills and purpose. It's unimportant that I sing (sort of) and cycle (slowly). But it's very important for you to see everyday dreams being created, time-pegged, and prioritized—and why. Because that's the path we're taking together to help you live a super life for many years to come, a life you design!

Enough apologies: you'll see my wife and me in the next chapter. There we ask what happens as you and your mate are simultaneously creating your own dream lists, time-pegging them, and each pulling your priorities to the top. How does that work for two?

When Super Second Life Dreams are Shared, Some Sifting and Sorting is Required

11

It's a double blessing having a partner, companion, or mate with whom you share your future.

There's the companionship, of course—maybe even love!

And there's the planning, which can be the source of great fun and mutual accomplishment. It will also be a challenge!

Our task in this chapter is to remove the negative aspects of that challenge by clearly identifying which dreams are singular and belong overwhelmingly to the dreamer and which either overlap with the other person or are wholly shared with them.

Something else important happens when you start comparing and merging shared dreams—you get to really talk with your mate about things that matter. Life-creating and life-confirming things.

Making sense for mated dreams and dreamers.

Independence and Interrelatedness

Many of us are married or have a partner and we intend to keep it that way for as long as we can.

But if you have a mate and that isn't so, why not just quickly skim this chapter to see what it says? (You've got other decisions to make and work to do that lies beyond the realm of this book. Come back here later, if it's appropriate.) But do continue to the next chapter and get your own Action Plan in order. You have valid dreams worth living.

125

The idea here is to see how we can take both our dreams and our partner's and create a shared Super Second Life where we each enjoy our independence *and* our desired interrelatedness for as long as possible.

The process begins by each of us developing our own Dream Lists, defining the dreams by commitment, then time-pegging them, as the previous chapters explained. Once we have completed our time-pegs, we can set them side-by-side to see which of our listed commitments are overlapping or shared and which are personal.

The two boxes that follow help us create those lists.

OVERLAPPING OR SHARED DREAMS / Date:	
(You)	(Your Partner)

PERSONAL DREAMS / Date:	
(You)	(Your Partner)

What goes in which box?

How do we determine which dreams go into which box?

Let me make a very loose assumption that explains one criterion. It is that most couples first pool their income(s) into a common, meets-the-needs kitty. From that kitty they pay their shared dreams too. Then what's left can be used for their personal, non-shared expenses or dreams. (See more about this in Chapter 14.)

So I would list in the "Overlapping and Shared Dreams" box three obvious items: (1) those dreams which would be jointly financed from pooled funds, (2) activities that are the same or very, very similar for both people, or (3) activities that, by their nature, make no sense without a companion. (Later we will use this box to produce a "Co-Funded Budget Sheet.")

All other dreams—those that are indeed individual to the respective mates—would go in the "Personal Dreams" box. (This box will later serve as the core of a "Personal Budget Sheet.")

Sometimes which goes where isn't all that clear. Like when mates will both be doing the same thing but the action is peculiar to each. For example, if both are cigar box jugglers and wish to continue that perilous and eccentric discipline into their rigidity, the issue is whether they (1) juggle as a team, (2) they both participate in the same large juggling group, or (3) they juggle separately, he with Field's Flying Objects and she with the Dainty Old Ladies Who Throw Things.

The first case is clearly shared. The third is purposely singular, or personal. But I have no idea about the second item. Alas, you are mates: talk and figure it out, then list appropriately. There are no iron-clad rules. It's your plan!

Your assignment now: compare your Dream Lists and fill in the two boxes.

A second example

Since we've focused primarily on my spine-tingling time-pegs, let's now take a first look my wife's prioritized, 55-70 time-peg. (You'll note that certain items are slightly reworded. They could be entirely reworded or different altogether since this entire process is dynamic and can be modified at any point or time.)

Neat places to visit...
Prussia
Constantinople
Ceylon
Baia
Belgian Congo
Indochina
Burma
Dodge City

TIME-PEG (1): 55-70 YEARS / Date: xxx Marsha Freeman Burgett
1. Have a warm, supportive, loving marriage.
2. Sell the publishing company.
3. Join forces with a leading consulting firm to sopify the dental world.
7. Maintain my weight at 125-130 pounds.
8. Be physically active through golf, walking, cycling, calisthenics, and sports.
9. Visit my family in Tulsa and Arkansas four times a year.
10. Visit my husband's daughters and family four times a year.
13. Interact with my children/grandchildren three to four times a week.
15. Surround myself with warm, supportive, creative, positive-minded people.
19. Read the daily paper and weekly/monthly periodicals.
26. Create a college trust fund for my grandchildren.
27. Buy a powerful laptop computer that will allow me to quickly access the Internet and to e-mail family and friends.
28. Have a positive impact on everyone I meet.
29. Become financially secure, wise, and responsible.
31. Go on an annual retreat with women friends.
35. Write a how-to standard operating procedures book for the masses.
37. Sightsee: visit historical sites, museums, art galleries, natural wonders.
40. Be brave, courageous, disciplined, principled, and ethical, and live a life of integrity and honesty.

Which dreams are shared?

Our next step is to transfer the appropriate dreams from her and my Dream Lists to the respective sides of the two boxes.

We'll see that in a moment, but something else very important is happening here, something every bit as significant as filling in the boxes. Since this is the first time we are seeing the other's prioritized Dream List, we are getting a unique, valuable look into the other's desires, hopes, and wants. And in comparing and discussing our lists, we are actually working together to create a new, shared dream for our joined future. That should strengthen any marriage at every step of the process.

This kind of structured, non-threatening future talk is rare to most marriages. Usually some general ideas are known or assumed and a general direction is understood as being shared but the details, breadth, and order are never discussed, much less put to paper.

Here, in a simple exercise, done separately and now brought together and compared, we can each see what is really important to the other person, what they care enough about to fight for. For us, it was a new insight into the other's expectations and fields of joy.

That sharing may be as important as the step-by-step planning of our collective and respective Super Second Lives.

What did our "Overlapping or Shared Dreams" box look like?

OVERLAPPING OR SHARED DREAMS / Date: xxx	
Gordon	Marsha
Remain happily married for our lives.	Have a warm, supportive, loving marriage.
Sell the DCU/MCU publishing firm.	Sell the publishing company.
See two live plays or concerts per month.	See two live plays or concerts per month.
Attend movies regularly.	Attend movies regularly.
Visit my daughters and their families at least quarterly.	Visit my husband's daughters and family four times a year.

In fact, it looks this way because of my highly tuned sensitivity and bountiful charity (salted with humility).

When Marsha first looked at my prioritized time-pegs, she cried unfair—"I'd have put them down too if I had thought of them!"—when she saw that I had included regularly seeing live plays, concerts, and movies. Ever the charmer, I simply included them in the shared box and added them to her side.

The other three were straightforward: we want to be together from here on (if you can imagine, she even wants warmth, support, and love!), we want to sell the publishing company (which we jointly created and own) so we can each move on, and we both want to visit my daughters and their spouses at least quarterly.

The number of shared dreams may vary

The number of our shared dreams was small, probably because we've only been married for five years and were single some years before during which we created full personal lives.

We decided to leave two other items on the separate, personal lists: controlling our respective finances and visiting her daughters regularly.

129

One thing is obvious, for you and us: since we are creating the list, we can decide where each dream goes and from which financial pot it will be financed.

Those dreams not in our "Overlapping or Shared Dreams" box go in the "Personal Dreams" box. We will see that list in Chapter 14.

As we discussed the items in that second box, I was surprised how strongly Marsha felt about visiting her folks (over a thousand miles away) four times a year. They are good people but the difficulty is the travel time required, the cost, and the length of the visits. Her wish is completely understandable since her parents are aging and unable to travel to us. And it will likely diminish as Marsha herself ages and her parents pass. But it also gave us a chance to reach some understanding about my own lack of enthusiasm for accompanying her on the trips, with a loose commitment to accompany her once a year to become better acquainted with her kin.

The rest was interesting to read but contained no shocking surprises for either of us.

What if we had found some real conflicts or areas of true discomfort? Like me wanting to burn bridges and she, build them? Or I detested her bevy of sisters and she wanted us both to live with each of them for two months every year? The conflict resolver in Chapter 15 would come into play. We have used it and while it's not magic, it sure comes close...

The point of this chapter is to identify now the directions and issues that will be important later, weigh their importance, and put those of merit on paper, to begin the dialog for resolution or a path for mutual enjoyment.

Better now than to find ourselves out to pasture and both running as fast as we can in different directions. Or worse, when one is running and the other is sitting.

So more planning and sorting on these pages. The future will come for couples or individuals whether we plan for it or not. Most us don't plan our first lives; we react. But we're older now, with learning and street smarts and living bruises. It makes nothing but sense to do it for the second time around.

Then the Dreams Must be Reduced to Specific Action Steps

12

Here is where the dreams gain form and grit. Where they are pounded into realizable shape so humans can work them into their everyday living. Here they get some flesh and bone—and legs.

At the dream level, "I want to leave a legacy, a lifelong imprint on young scientists (or wayward teens, ...)" works just fine. It's properly imposing, lofty in direction, worthy of sacrifice, suitably vague. It inspires even the dreammaker as it's said or read. It makes the spirit soar and promises wee threads of immortality.

Alas, dreams needn't be that exalted. "Organizing a regular family Easter reunion" or "an uninterrupted hour a day to read" are no less valuable or dreamworthy.

But none of them really mean much without some additional hard thinking and planning and commitment. Most need some action retooling. Which is what this chapter is about. It explains a process and means to bring the highest goals to doable steps so they reach the action plan in workable form.

Dreams are hopes; they live in the mind and spirit. Actions are things done with the hands and the mind. We need both, but it's the doing that brings us the kinds of results (and those wisps of immortality) that can make a Super Second Life truly super. Unless we curl up right now, we all get a second life. The magic is in the doing.

Hands-on work here, developing an action list by converting dreams into people-sized, real world steps.

---

*Dicing dreams
into edible bites*

What makes dreams so hard to embrace and live is that they are so distant, so misty, so grand. It's hard to scale the face of a mountain, but no great task to climb a series of small hills.

So here we reduce the imprecise dreams to very precise steps, so that we know their components and, by knowing them, how we can make those dreams come true.

One example will show what we've all experienced, that of putting something off and off because it seemed like so much work and we didn't quite know how to begin.

Some years back I was offering workshops to professionals who wanted to create and program their own seminars, some publicly but most to be sponsored by colleges or other institutions. Some time during the middle of the program a hand would go up and a daring soul would ask, "How do I make audio cassettes to sell to the people who attend my seminar?" I particularly remember it because I wanted to do exactly the same thing but hadn't the foggiest notion how. So I responded, "I'm about to do the same thing. I'll leave a sheet of legal paper on the back table. If any of you would like to know the process, put down your name and address and I'll let you know the precise steps —by audio cassette!"

Once I had gathered some of those legal pad pages, the clock was ticking. I had to live up to my promise.

So what I did was make two lists for my own use: one included everything I knew (almost nothing) about the process plus everything I could deduce by looking at singles and cassette series. The second list included every question I needed answered to be able to decipher the process and make it doable by others as ignorant as myself.

"Money is time."

George Gissing

I then trotted off to the library—those were pre-web times—and dug into the reference sources for anything I could find about audio cassette preparation, production, and sale. There was shockingly little. Worse than little. After you removed the unintelligible electronics articles, there was nothing. Except the names of duplicators and some product reviews of tape machines for home use. (Remember, audio cassettes were still fairly new at that time.)

The instructions for the tape recorders were minimally helpful. But the companies that did the duplication had the answers—and wanted you to know them, so they would have something to duplicate! So I made an appointment with three duplicators (since I would need duplication of my tapes as soon as I could figure what to say on them and how to package them). They gave me reams of how-to advice and costs, plus addresses and phone numbers about where to buy V-cards, Norelco plastic boxes, labels, and mailers.

"Prepare to live by all means, but for Heaven's sake do not forget to live."

Arnold Bennett

I bought an inexpensive tape deck, figured out how to connect it to my amplifier, where to plug in the microphone, how to position its holder to reduce unwanted noise, and how to get my voice recorded. It took hours of toying to get a good master, and hours more to order the right packaging components. But a month later the mountain was scaled, and my first (and still best single selling) audio was created: "Producing and Selling Your Own Audio Cassettes."

Which is the long way to say, I had a dream but it was just that. It only became a reality (and a very profitable, long-term income font) when I broke it down into its doable parts, then reassembled them so they fit my peculiar needs.

That's what we must do now with our dreams. We must define each by the steps we must take, now or later, to make the dream doable. And in the cases where we are already doing part of that dream, how we can do it better or in a way compatible with our later vision.

Put your ideas down on paper

Of all the steps we take in this book, this will probably seem the least necessary. "I'll just do it when the time comes," you say. "If I can do it now, I can do it then—and anyway, in this fast-changing world it will probably be all different when I'm one or many decades older. Right now it seems like just so much busywork."

I hear you—and flat-out disagree, although you're probably right that you will have to adjust your actions later to match the changes that will take place in the meantime.

None of us really likes change. And we're very, very slow about doing new things—a tendency that almost always gets worse as we age. So if we don't break down the process barriers now, many or even most of our dreams will probably remain as far from our everyday activities as they are today.

133

"Growing old is
something you do if
you're lucky."

Groucho Marx

That's the key reason that this book needs Chapter 15. It explains a tool for conflict resolution that also helps reduce resistance and inertia. The largest part of that tool is micro-defining the dream: breaking it into understandable and easily doable parts, which is what we're doing now.

There's a powerful second reason too. If your dreams are so great, why wait until you're 60 or 80 to do them? Why not get started now, at least learning the rudiments or buying the utensils? Getting a head start is far easier if you understand the basics of the dream first.

I recall reading about a bored high school sophomore who was ordered by his mother to take his grandfather fishing. He moaned and moped but finally agreed, mostly because he needed an adult in the car so he could drive. The boy had never baited a worm—nor, amazingly, had the grandfather! But they had a lot of fun, caught some fish, and set up a weekly date to fish out all of the local lakes and ponds. I remember the article because the boy boasted to all his friends that he'd taught his grandfather how to fish—and that he wasn't going to lose 60 years of fun like his gramps had!

The specifics

How much must each dream be broken into its doing parts? It varies.

If a future dream is already part of your routine and you intend to continue on in the same fashion into future time-pegs, there's really nothing to add except as it affects future changes.

But if it's fishing and you aren't sure if they fly or grunt, then there may be a dozen things to list and look at in this phase. As a rule, the less familiar and the larger the dream is, the more detail it may require.

Let's create the first part of an Action Plan now, calling it an Action Step Worksheet, adding the five Ws and H of journalism here as starter tools to help you remember the basics when you fill it out. Those are who, what, why, where, when, and how. You ask each about those dreams you wish to itemize or further define. Some may not apply. Others may require many answers.

The insert with the dollar sign indicates financial impact. Let's leave that blank until the next chapter. As we go along we will continue to add new components to this Action Plan, until it emerges in final form.

ACTION STEP WORKSHEET	
Name:	
Dream:	**$**
Action Steps : [Who, what, why, where, when, and how?]	

Let me isolate four examples to provide a rough idea of what is needed to put dreams on a realization track. (My difficulty in finding more than four is that I'm actually doing the rest, being 61 with a list planned for that time. If I had 10-15 years between the planning and execution, I'd have a lot more that needed greater definition now!)

These are the four, with the first limited to one of the two publishing firms since either they are so interwoven they will sell as a unit or the process for selling the unsold firm would be essentially the same. I will focus on speaking to associations in the third example and on swimming my age at 62 in the fourth, both somewhat modified from the Dreams List to save your time.

2. Sell the D.C.U. / M.C.U. publishing firm.
3. Phase out my C.U. publishing firm, probably between ages 65-70.
5. Speak to associations, corporations, other groups about Super Second Life, 2-3 times a month until about 68 (or it isn't fun).
20. Continue my Agemasters achievements as long as possible: cycle my age in miles (then kms); attempt to swim my age in kms; at 62 run my age in kms; add in walking my age later.

In the first example, D.C.U. means Dental Communication Unlimited. We produce niched items for dentists (and staff), mostly printed standard operating procedures manuals (in three-ring binder format, each book accompanied by a computer disk). The company also sells video and audio cassettes, bound books, and reports. My purpose here is to delineate what I must do to make this sale happen.

Dream: Sell the D.C.U. publishing firm.	**$**

Action Steps : [Who, what, why, where, when, and how?]

1. Create a current business plan projected five years into the future.
2. Contact a publishing sales broker with experience in the dental and medical field.
3. Work with the broker to create an acquisition prospectus.
4. With the broker, help create a potential buyer list.
5. Bring all accounting records up-to-date and maintain them on a weekly updated basis.
6. Accelerate the collection of all accounts receivable.
7. Accelerate efforts to sell current inventory, focusing on the "hot" and in-house customer list.
8. Reduce book printing and disk duplication to stock needed for 3-6 months.
9. Stop all building modification, vehicle purchases, or other long-term expansion.
10. Replace employees strictly on an as-needed basis.
11. Double efforts to keep the firm fully operating during the sales transition.
12 Work with the broker, lawyer, and accountant when purchase offers are made.
13. Work with the accountant on the use of funds and equity received from the purchase.
14. Dispose of items and holdings not in the purchase agreement.

The second Action Plan concerns an older publishing and seminaring firm, called C.U. (or Communication Unlimited). It existed before our expansion into the dental and medical fields, and has become a passive, secondary income font, especially since my seminar- and speech-giving was reduced from as many as 120 a year to about 35 at the present. It now consists of a half-dozen book titles in print, 15 audio cassettes and series, a manuscript evaluation program, and seminar and speaking programs. It will simply cease to function when I do, so my action plan is, likewise, rather passive, except where it refers to the Super Second Life program.

What Are You Going to Do With Your Extra 30 Years?

Dream: Phase out my C.U. publishing firm, probably between ages 65-70.	**$**

Action Steps : [Who, what, why, where, when, and how?]

1. Maintain the firm as is until I quit seminaring at the university level, in a year or two.
2. In the meantime, purge the large mailing list of outdated listings.
3. Study a one-time, cut-rate sale of all C.U. products in a last mailing.
4. Find a remaindering house to buy the unsold C.U. books.
5. Reduce the production of cassettes to an on-order basis, using an in-house duplicator.
6. Bring all accounting records up-to-date and maintain them on a weekly update basis.
7. Sell or license writing and publishing seminars to another person or firm.
8. Sell equipment and stock, as it becomes unnecessary for C.U. activities.
9. Redirect employee(s) from publishing to the Super Second Life program: promotion, booking, travel, back-of-room supplies (if appropriate), liaison.
10. After books and seminaring are over, decide whether to keep this structure to house the Super Second Life activities or switch it entirely to Agemasters.

Since I anticipate significant demand for speaking related to the book you are reading, that must be planned for and built into my coming years. As indicated above, I have staff already experienced in the logistics and correspondence related to seminars and speeches, so what I need now is a starting structure to launch the workshops and keynotes, then a base to continue it until the demand withers or I do.

Dream: Speak to associations 2-3 times a month until about 68 (or it isn't fun).	**$**

Action Steps : [Who, what, why, where, when, and how?]

1. Work with the publisher to create maximum book and author exposure.
2. Create a national book tour, to maximize radio and TV contacts.
3. Keep listings in media reference publications and websites current; use them often.
4. Work with publisher to maximize library purchases.
5. Develop three Super Second Life core presentations: keynote, 1-2 hour, and 4-hour workshop.
6. Keep testing the workshop at university sites in California.
7. Create the visuals needed for each format: workbook, slide, and computer-projected.
8. Begin bookings through familiar dental/medical associations, with customized program.
9. Locate other associations and set up an office-driven booking campaign.
10. Talk with NSA colleagues about specific marketing targets.
11. Investigate creation of second and third book follow-ups, with publisher or through C.U.
12. Put the key information on an audio cassette series, with workbook, geared to libraries.
13. Create a video program based on the book concept and visuals.
14. Investigate the feasibility of Super Second Life clubs or organizations.

So far, it's been all about work, though speaking is joyous work. I'd like to subject my too-quickly booming body to some severe hardship, in part to stay fit and in part to scold it for gaining so much weight so soon. Mostly, though, because I like the exercise, enjoy the occasional solitude, and feel better after I feel worse. The specific case in point: can I swim my age at 62? Since I have an option in my Agemasters program of doing so in miles or kilometers (about 6/10s of a mile), I pick the latter! Which means I would have to swim 62 kilometers (38.5 miles) in 62 days or less, averaging one kilometer a day. Here's how I might do that:

Dream: Continue my Agemasters achievements as long as possible: attempt to swim my age at 62 in kilometers.	**$**

Action Steps : [Who, what, why, where, when, and how?]

1. Start as early after 6/17/00 as possible, in case I goof up. That will give me another 60-day time slot in the same age bracket.
2. Have the doctor check out the left shoulder to see the kind of damage this could create.
3. If that's acceptable, set aside 60 inviolate days where I would be able to swim. Since it occasionally rains here from November to about April and the pool is outdoors, I might avoid those months, if my schedule allows.
4. Increase my swimming regimen to three days a week three months before the starting date, and expand from a half-mile swim to a full mile the first and third day each week. If the back or shoulder act up, pull back to a half mile and save the pain for the event.
5. Reduce the swimming to two 3/4-mile swims a week the month before.
6. From the first day on, plan to swim six days a week: one mile the first and last of the six (presuming Sunday is the rest day); 3/4 mile the second, fourth, and fifth day, and five-eighths of a mile on the third.
7. That will give me a half-mile buffer (or extra) should I miss a day.
8. I would prefer to simply add an extra eighth of a mile on the third day and create an extra mile buffer to add to that half mile, allowing for a two-day absence if necessary.
9. That presumes that, particularly in the beginning, if I do miss a day the loss must be made up over the next four or five days, to keep the goal clearly in view and doable.
10. I will verify with the YMCA where I swim if they will still have the three lap times available—5-7 am, 11-2, and 4-7—so if it gets difficult I can break the daily swim into two or three parts. Otherwise I will plan to swim at one time a day, probably around noon.
11. I'll talk with the swim coach about modifying my diet, if needed, around that time.
12. I'll experiment with ear plugs and a swimming cap, the former to reduce "swimmer's ear."

13. I will reduce or eliminate golf those eight weeks, and check with a trainer to see which other exercises are advisable to offset the swimming. Will eliminate or reduce the running, and will cycle locally if I feel like it.
14. Will get my wife's support and cooperation.
15. Will post my daily distances on the Y wall chart, as a form of double-check.
16. On the 60th day, two days early, when I finish the 62K swim, I'll come home and post it with Agemasters, then we'll go out that night and celebrate!

You get the idea? The more we break these down now into digestible bites, the more likely we will enjoy the feast later.

At the least, defining small, doable steps keeps us from foot shuffling and procrastination, then roiling in emotional and mental paralysis, then muddling in remorse after the fact because we did nothing.

On the more immediate and less dramatic side, it also helps us identify the financial impact each dream will create. And just in time, since that's what we must do next, in Chapter 13.

No man should fret in case his hair
Turns silver in his prime
He's fortunate that some was there
To turn at turning time.

William W. Pratt

Financial Resources Must Now be Added to the Action Plan

13

In the real world, dreams and plans aren't executed in a vacuum. They almost always have economic consequences: they cost money to do, they take time that might be used to earn rather than spend capital, and they use money that might be used for something else...

In Chapter 7 we devised a worksheet to see when we might have dispensable money available at various times during your Super Second Life. Here is where that money is matched up with the things you want to use it for.

"Isn't this a bit like balancing 'maybe' dreams with 'perchance' cash?" you ask. "How can that be done with any kind of precision 15 or 30 years away, with 150 variables in between?"

Of course it's imprecise but the goals and the approximate budgets at least provide a general framework within which a future direction can be plotted and necessary financial decisions can now be made to help make the best of that future happen. Without planning, not only do the variables lack bias, no coordinated, orderly energy is created to positively direct your future.

Anyway, the plan and the financial links can be changed any day of your life—but you must first know them to make that change. So we start now...

Here we match your plans with your ability to afford them.

Alas, nothing's free

No brain surgery required here. By the age of 40 or 50 you've learned one of the hardest lessons of life: nothing's free, including lunch. The future is no exception, though it's a bit freer with senior discounts for, it seems, nearly everything but senior services.

So we must find out now if we will be able to afford our geriatric vices, or if we will be limited to the thinnest pastures of the good life for want of moolah.

Future money will probably come from three sources: (1) money we or our employers have saved for us, (2) money we will earn during those years, or (3) surprise money, like an inheritance or your kids paying back their childhood allowances, probably in the same weekly increments. Just so it doesn't come with the same spending directives: "Don't buy anything stupid with this!" or "Be sure to put half of this in your college fund!"

"Money is that which gives a man thirty years more of dignity."

Chinese proverb

We spoke in Chapter 7 about building the necessary financial base to give you choices and some pecuniary freedom in your dotage.

This is where we take a look, again, at our final Super Second Life Money Worksheet for the various time-pegs to see, approximately, how much we have available to spend.

At the same time we must make a rough calculation of how much it will cost to fulfill our dreams. The latter we will include in the "$" box in the many Action Plans from each time-peg bracket. (Those boxes are the source of the "Special super life expenses this year" in the Worksheet.)

When our wants exceed our means...

If our needs are less than our ability to pay with discretionary funds, great.

If we want more than we can afford, we have several choices:

(1) We can want less—reducing the number of dreams or allocating less to each.
(2) We can postpone them to a later time or age bracket. But there can be a problem if we do that for too long!

(3) We can earn some or all of our shortfall funds, probably by part-time working.

(4) We can find a way to reduce the costs of realizing one or many of the wants, to be able to afford more with less.

We'll see examples of each of these in a moment.

Finally, we will follow a similar procedure for those items shared by mates, except that here we have an added nuisance. If there's a shortfall, we must decide which of the two will have to do the dream trimming, if it comes to that! (Here, the one who lives longest really may get the last laugh.)

Let me use six examples, my four itemized in the last chapter plus two more shared by my wife and I. It's not necessary to see the itemized steps in each case, so we'll use just the top sections of the respective Action Plans, expanded.

Dream: Sell my D.C.U. publishing firm.	**$**
	N.A.

This item is inapplicable (N.A.) because it directly relates to and is financed by my business. The results of the sale—particularly the amount of net profit and when it will be available in some liquid form—will, of course, affect my future spendable assets, but the costs of getting the firm ready for sale, the selling, and the related after-costs had not yet been allocated to my retirement spending fund. My interest here is to see that the net profits are as high as possible and accessible when needed.

Assuming I can live as I wish, within reason, until the firm sells, the timing is as important as the amount. My preference is to sell it now, while I'm still alive and have the days to enjoy the results of the labor and energy spent earning it.

For those not selling a firm or self-employed, this is the same as determining when you leave your primary occupation and cash in your retirement. You will want to figure what exit date is most suitable for you to receive the highest return accessible when you need it.

Dream: Phase out my C.U. publishing firm, probably between ages 65-70.	$
	N.A.

Again, a business decision that will cost me no saved income, though it will directly affect my future earnings. Since the holdings here are much smaller and the inventory is aging and has relatively little resale value other than to a niched clientele mostly reached by my seminars, workshops, and mailing list, the steps listed to continue the seminars for about two years (in part to sell inventory back of the room), to conduct a one-time total list clearance sale, to remainder anything I can, and to stop stocking other than on an order-only basis can be done at my own pace since the cost of warehousing is minimal and the entire operation can be conducted by one paid employee, with me limited to offering the seminars and workshops.

When the costs of the employee and remaining expenses exceed the income generated, I will simply close the door and sell, donate, or dispose of the physical holdings.

The alternative is to meld the diminishing C.U. operations into the new speech and workshop activities generated by the Super Second Life presentations, use the same office equipment and staff, and continue until that runs out of steam or I do.

In the first case, there will be no expenditures from my allocated retirement fund, so I can afford to slowly and quietly fold C.U. without creating any financial distress. Let's discuss the latter case in the next Action Plan, since that may be run through the present C.U. structure.

Dream: Speak to associations 2-3 times a month about Super Second Life concept, until I'm about 68 (or it isn't fun).	$
	$2,500

Here there can be some financial risk, so caution must be exercised.

But the income that can be generated from incurring that initial risk can be so large that its overall negative affect, or drain, on my allocated retirement fund is slight if nonexistent. In fact, it should bring in plenty of profit to help finance other Super Second Life dreams.

As an example of how you might quickly calculate a similar Action Plan, add a new segment below the Action Steps to include those steps that cost cash or earn income. Also create two columns on the right: COSTS and POTENTIAL INCOME. (Calculations include labor, if done by an employee, and incidentals.)

ACTION STEP WORKSHEET

Name: Gordon Burgett

Dream: Speak to associations 2-3 times a month about Super Second Life concept, until I'm about 68 (or it isn't fun).	COSTS	POTENTIAL INCOME
1. I find potential markets at library or through web: associations	$ 50	$ 0
2. Create a speaking packet: folder, inserts, business card. Have 500 produced at $3 each.	1,500	0
3. Create, send initial two-sided introductory letter to 500 bookers.	375	0
4. Mail the packet, as requested, to bookers. Send USPS 2-3 day.	500-1,700	0
5. If requested, include demo tapes in stock. $2.40 each. (150)	380	0
6. Create video demos from early SSL presentations. (100 copies)	2,500	0
7. I follow up each request by phone or e-mail, 1X - 3X	150	0
8. Employee calls non-responding bookers, mostly 1X	1,000	0
9. Handle unsolicited requests, from book / book-related radio-TV	650	0
10. Book 2 workshops a month at $3,000@, plus one speech $2,500	0	8,500 / mth
	$ 7,705	$ 8,500

Finally, good news!

The good news is that one month's booking (two workshops and a speech) will pay for all the marketing, and make most of the future very, very rosy.

The bad news is the first $7,705 (say $8,000) is needed for the booking. It's possible that nobody will want to hear me wax ecstatic about planning for a Super Second Life and I will end up with a large $1,500 box of folders. Of course, if only a few want me to mail the folder out, I save some postage. And if nobody books me, there will be no video since I plan to make the master at an early presentation.

Most of the other expenses would be lower too. So if it turns out to be a turkey supremo (which is what I usually eat), that $8,000 in costs will be closer to $2,500. Then the question is, do I have $2,500 in mad money to book myself? Since the early bookers will put half on deposit to hold the date, I will bring in a fairly fast $3,500 or so to add to my $2,500—and most of the remaining $2,000 (actually $2,500 needed for a video) will come later at booked presentations. So let's put $2,500 in the Itemized Action Plan box.

I admit that this is quick figuring and a bit loose logically to come to these totals, but having been a speaker for 20+ years, the numbers aren't far off. (Nor do I advocate that one emulate this booking procedure, but it works for me.)

Does it fit into my Super Second Life plan? We'll look at all of the items in the next chapter to see, but at least we now have a usable cost to make that consideration at that time.

Let's use this example to test the four approaches we might use if we didn't have the $2,500 in discretionary funds for this activity. How might we be able to afford this speaking venture?

(1) We can want less—reducing the number of dreams or allocating less to each. *Simple enough: cut this one out, or something else, so we have the available $2,500.*

(2) We can postpone them to a later time or age bracket. *My next age bracket starts at 70, a ripe old age to be traveling the country, eating bad food, and standing for four hours giving workshops. After about 65 or so it gets tough, so I'd want it to be going by then if at all. If I had to postpone it a couple of years, fine, but not much longer. Nothing sadder than seeing your keynoter babble and drool—if it's unintended.*

(3) We can earn some or all of our shortfall funds, probably by part-time working. *That's a better idea. I'll just keep giving my regular seminars and throw a dozen Super Second Life ones into the mix, which will get me bookings from those participants. That way I can afford the regular booking format and keep the presentation, at least in workshop form, active and improving.*

(4) We can find a way to reduce the costs of realizing one or many of the wants, to be able to afford more with less. *Focusing solely on the costs here, I can forget the audio and video demos and the follow-up phoning, save $3,880, and it might work just fine. But the approach is already thin and no demos make a hard sell through bureaus or to sophisticated markets.*

Dream: Continue my Agemasters achievements as long as possible: attempt to swim my age at 62 in kilometers.	**$**
	$ 567

This one is easy and affordable. I swim at the local YMCA which charges seniors $22 a month ($264 a year), if you bring your own towel and promise not to drown. Add to that a bit of driving expense the days I don't cycle the five miles ($263), a new swim suit ($20) and goggles ($10) every six months or so, and a few bucks for medication to slow down "swimmer's ear" ($10), and I come up with $567 a year. Since I'd have to swim a couple of years to reach that goal at 62, that might cost me $1,000 or so until that is achieved.

What would happen if I never swam the 62 kilometers? I'd be fit, have fun, and keep out of trouble. And if I didn't swim I'd probably spend it some other way, if it was available. So the real question is, "Do I want to swim regularly for the next two years?" If so, that'll cost at most $1,000.

When you and your mate both have travel expenses?

While each item generates its own Action Plan, on the next page let's look at two at the same time in print to see how each of us plans for our own travel costs.

These amounts assume that we each book several weeks in advance, spend Saturday night there, fly coach, rent small compact cars, and the kin provide a bed and some of our victuals.

Again, there are ways to reduce these amounts:

(1) We can want less—reducing the number of realized dreams or allocating less to each. *Of course, we can just eliminate one or several trips. We can mooch a car from the family when we arrive. We can drive less or rent the car for fewer days when we're there. They can visit us.*

ACTION STEP WORKSHEET		ACTION STEP WORKSHEET	
Dreams: Travel annually to see brothers, in alternate years.		Visit family in Tulsa and Arkansas four times a year.	
GORDON	COSTS	MARSHA	COSTS
1. Round-trip to Hagerstown, MD	$ 602	1. Round-trip to Tulsa	$ 410
2. Car rental for one week	175	2. Car rental for one week, to drive to Arkansas	175
3. Gas money for rental	20	3. Gas money for rental	45
4. Mad money during visit	200	4. Mad money during visit	175
5. Round-trip to St. Louis, MO	510		
6. Car rental for one week	140		
7. Gas money for rental	35		
8. Mad money during visit	150		
Trip to Maryland	$ 997	One trip to Tulsa/Arkansas	$ 805
Trip to St. Louis	$ 835	Four trips to Tulsa/Arkansas	$ 3,220

(2) We can postpone them to a later time or age bracket. *That's okay with my brothers, but Marsha's mother won't be around if we delay too long.*

(3) We can earn some or all of our shortfall funds, probably by part-time working. *Better yet, in this case, we can include the trips as add-ons to our speaking itinerary, if we are still doing that and are booked in the general area. Logistically, the speaking sponsor pays to get us to their site and we pay for the flight diversion or the rate is divided equally— either way, both make a savings.*

(4) We can find a way to reduce the costs of realizing one or many of the wants, to be able to afford more with less. *Those pesky Frequent Flyer miles gathered while speaking can pay for the airfare and the rental car, so this may be a zero cost outlay at least during our last working years. (After our working years there may be less reason or will to travel as often.) We can also drive to Los Angeles (175 miles each way) and considerably reduce the air fares (offset some by the parking fees.)*

But when the expenses come from a common money font and the action is equally desired by both, then a slightly different form, the "Joined Action Step Worksheet," is appropriate.

JOINED ACTION STEP WORKSHEET	
Names:	
Joined Dream: Visit Gordon's daughters / families four times a year.	$ 600
Car travel, $30 x 4	$ 120
Food, $95 x 4	$380
Motel, $50 x 2	$100

The above numbers are based on the fact that both daughters, recently married, live in fairly close proximity so overnighting is only a consideration in one case. This also presumes that they will come to visit us about half the time. And, bless them, that I will still be paying for a meal out at each visit. How might the above look, with details?

"Middle age is when everything starts to wear out, fall out or spread out."

Why bother to list the costs when the plans are long from becoming reality? Because we must start budgeting somewhere with solid numbers, and being mortals we will have no idea where the odd totals came from or how they were derived. It's far easier to modify than try to conjure up lost ciphers.

"Life without love is a bird without a song. Life without trust is a night without day. Life without faith is a tree without root. Life without hope is a year without Spring. Life without friends is a sun without shade. Life without work is a bloom without fruit."

Dr. William Arthur Ward

The Final Action Plan | 14

It took long enough, didn't it? Why not just jot down some goals, tack them to the refrigerator, and knock off one every year or so? Sounds good to me!

Except it's too little and too vague to cover a 30- or 40-year span. And you don't get a second chance at a second life—it ticks off irretrievably with or without a plan.

So why not inject extra brain and elbow grease now, take all you've done, and put it in final form? (Not that you can't tinker with it later or even throw it out and start again. But you must have an actual Final Action Plan at some point, to use or toss. This is it.)

This chapter expands on what that means, what a Final Action Plan to a Super Second Life might look like, where you might put it (your friends may have suggestions!), and who should know about it. Mostly, though, here you complete your own plan!

At last, in writing and ready to implement: a Super Second Life Final Action Plan!

From dreams to life plans

It all started with a conviction, that we *could* plan, then create our own second life.

But to define the way that we wanted that life to be, we had to first imagine it, then give words to that image. Those words we captured on a Dream List.

Alas, some dreams are too ephemeral to gain substance, others are passing whims, a few are even born of envy. Still, among that batch are core dreams that truly exemplify our spirit, that capture the kind of person and style of life we want. We'll do what it takes to make *those* dreams come true.

We were then asked to separate those top-commitment dreams and put them into time-pegs so they matched our wishes and needs when we are ready and able to live them.

Then we gave legs to those dreams, or at least the newest and most ambitious of them, by creating action steps that would help put them in motion.

And finally we had to figure out the cost (or profit) of enacting those dreams, to see if or how they might fit into our future financial reality.

In this chapter, all of those steps are brought together into a Final Action Plan, to which we will add two new segments, "Health Considerations" and "Preparatory Actions."

Later, we will create a final set of time-peg forms that will help evaluate all of our dreams' affordability.

The Final Action Plan: a blueprint, guide, and map

The purpose of this chapter and book is to create just enough paper structure to build the dreams into existence when and as planned. The Final Action Plan becomes our blueprint, reference guide, and map in one.

On the next page we see a blank Final Action Plan.

Bringing all of our thinking and doodling into one Final Action Plan allows us to see all of the major planning considerations at one time. We put the dream into words, which means we define it into usable form. We break it down into the steps needed to give that dream active structure; that is, we tell what we must do to make it come true. Third, we roughly calculate the financial impact the dream will have in terms of costing or generating money (or both).

Then we hark back to Chapter 6 and consider the health implications. Those can be logistical or economic. If we were lame and planned to descend to the bottom of the Grand Canyon, then climb back up, there would indeed be health considerations: (1) is it doable at all? (2) is it doable now while we can still barely walk, but highly unlikely in the coming years?

(3) do we need special equipment or medication? (4) would it be more prudent to take the mule trip down and back?

FINAL ACTION PLAN / Time-Peg - / Date:		
Dream:		**$**

ACTION STEPS

FINANCIAL CALCULATIONS	COSTS	POTENTIAL INCOME
	$	$
TOTALS	$	$

HEALTH CONSIDERATIONS

PREPARATORY ACTIONS

Some of those would be addressed in the "Health Considerations" section, others in the actual action steps, so their economic impact could be included.

The last segment, "Preparatory Actions," refers to either those things we might or wish to do before the time-peg arrives to realize this dream—or have already done. (In the latter case, I'd simply indicate that it was done and when.)

Expanding on the example just posed, if we plan to take the mule trek in, say, three years but have never been atop anything more reactionary than a chair, we may wish to (1) go riding for an hour at a local stable, (2) increase that to two hours, then longer subsequent rides, (3) attend a travelogue about the mule trip given at the nearby junior college, and (4) read about the Grand Canyon. Completing this section reminds us of the things we can start doing now to make our future endeavors even more enjoyable.

Which dreams would require preparing a Final Action Plan? I'd do them all at this crucial stage of planning, if for no other reason than it forces me to think about all facets of each idea, however uncomplicated or free it is. Moreover, I'd do it at every time-peg.

But if that seems overkill to you, then I'd prepare a full Final Action Plan for at least those dreams that you have the least experience with, the most ambitious, and those with many action steps, financial implications, health considerations, or that can be started before the time-peg for the dream's initial or fullest realization.

Is that it, then? We can rev up and kick back for the Super Second Life?

Yes, if you are so rich that no dream is beyond your means.

For the rest of us, one last step is prudent if not mandatory. We should put our Final Action Plans into time-peg piles (again, in my case, one pile for the time-peg from 60-70, another for 70-80, and the last for 81+). For each, we should then prepare separate time-pegged Super Second Life Money Worksheets, to see how we can finance as many of these dreams as possible—or more!

We need a Money Worksheet first

It all starts with the Super Second Life Money Worksheet we prepared in Chapter 7 because we need to know at the outset how much dispensable money we have to finance our dreams. What might that completed sheet look like?

Super Second Life Money Worksheet: Age—65 / Date: xxx			
Annual basic living expenses		(A)	$ 40,000
Annual basic income:			
Annual Social Security income	$ 28,000		
Annual pension income	$ 22,000		
Other annual income: Royalties	$ 14,000		
Other annual income:	$		
Other annual income:	$		
Total income	(add totals above)	(B)	$ 64,000
Annual basic income deficit/surplus	(A) - (B)	(C)	$ + 24,000
Monthly supplemental income needed	÷12		$ 0
Special super life expenses this year	(from Action Plan)	(D)	$ 20,000
Total money desired for this year	(A) + (D)		$ 60,000
Maximum income deficit/surplus	if C is -, (C) + (D)		
	if C is +, (C) - (D)	(E)	$ + 4,000
Monthly supplemental income needed	÷12		$ 0
Additional income source(s):	Amount		
Income source:	$		
Income source:	$		
Income source:	$		
Income source:	$		
Income source:	$		
Income source:	$		
Additional income available this year	$	(F)	
Total income deficit/surplus for this year	C + F		$ + 24,000

The crucial number is found in (C), a surplus of $24,000. In the example that follows, we decided to use only $20,000 of that ($10,000 for me and the same for my wife). The $4,000 surplus in (E) means that after deducting our $20,000, we still have a surplus, which we will leave in interest-earning securities.

The availability of funds now established, the Final Action Plan itself looks like the other forms we've been using, except all pulled together. In fact, this example includes the steps we have already seen describing how I might be able to speak about this Super Second Life topic to associations, plus the initial costs I might incur to make this dream come true.

FINAL ACTION PLAN / Time-Peg 60-70 / Date: xxx	
Dream: Speak to associations 2-3 times a month about Super Second Life concept, until I'm about 68 (or it isn't fun).	**$ 2,500**

ACTION STEPS

1. Work with the publisher to create maximum book and author exposure.
2. Create a national book tour, to maximize radio and TV contacts.
3. Keep listings in media reference publications and websites current; use them often.
4. Work with publisher to maximize library purchases.
5. Develop three Super Second Life core presentations: keynote, 1-2 hour, and workshop, 4.
6. Keep testing the workshop at university sites in California.
7. Create the visuals needed for each format: workbook, slide, and computer-projected.
8. Begin bookings through familiar dental/medical associations, with customized program.
9. Locate other associations and set up an office-driven booking campaign.
10. Talk with NSA colleagues about specific marketing targets.
11. Investigate creation of second and third book follow-ups, with publisher or through C.U.
12. Put the key information on an audio cassette series, with workbook, geared to libraries.
13. Create a video program based on the book concept and visuals.
14. Investigate the feasibility of Super Second Life clubs or organizations.

FINANCIAL CALCULATIONS	COSTS	POTENTIAL INCOME
1. I find potential markets at library or through web: associations	$ 50	$ 0
2. Create a speaking packet: folder, inserts, business card. Have 500 produced at $3 each.	1,500	0
3. Create, send initial two-sided introductory letter to 500 bookers.	375	0
4. Mail the packet, as requested, to bookers. Send USPS 2-3 day.	500-1,700	0
5. If requested, include demo tapes in stock. $2.40 each. (150)	380	0
6. Create video demos from early SSL presentations. (100 copies)	2,500	0
7. I follow up each request by phone or e-mail, 1X - 3X	150	0
8. Employee calls non-responding bookers, mostly 1X	1,000	0
9. Handle unsolicited requests, from book / book-related radio-TV	650	0
10. Book 2 workshops a month at $3,000@, plus one speech $2,500	0	8,500 / mth
TOTALS	$ 7,705	$ 8,500

HEALTH CONSIDERATIONS

1. None at present. Am physically and mentally fit and vigorous.
2. In future, rigors of travel, logistics, standing long periods of time, memory loss.

PREPARATORY ACTIONS

1. Have begun marketing in dental field, and have a booking in Hawaii in March, 2000.
2. Am currently printing new speaking packet binder, business cards.
3. Will assemble new inserts in speaking packet in July, 1999.
4. Building on 20 years of professional speaking, no additional training necessary.
5. Will begin contacting associations in August, 1999.
6. Booked three SSL programs at CA universities in fall of 1999.

Time-Peg
Budget Sheets

"Maturity is not being taken in by oneself."
Katjetan von Schlaggenberg

We'll talk about what we do with (and where we keep) these Final Action Plans in a moment, but two things are missing. Listing the specific actions by time-peg and then figuring out how we're going to pay for these dreams!

That's the job of the two Time-Peg Budget Sheets, one for singles, the other for pairs. Their purpose is straightforward, to list all of the things you want to do in a set time period, tally their cost, compare that with the funds you have at your call during that period, and breathe easy or make adjustments!

Let's first look at a Budget Sheet for singles since even mates will prepare these for the activities that are paid for by their own, or discretionary, funds. The sample that follows is three years wide, because of the book space limitations, though most time-pegs are a decade or longer. So your actual Budget Sheet may have a topic column followed by 10 or 15 more, each for a specific year. Those can be produced by computer but that usually requires special paper and "landscape" printing. Most stationary stores sell accounting columnar pads ideal for just this exercise. The model "singles" sheet is called the "Personal Budget Sheet." An example is seen on the next page.

If we have four time-pegs, we could list the respective dreams of each period on its own sheet, with, as noted, a column for each year in that time-peg. In each column we would write the estimated amount it would cost annually to implement that dream (even if there are no expenses involved).

PERSONAL BUDGET SHEET TIME-PEG ( ): Years - / Date:			
Dreams:	2001	2002	2003
Funds available after co-funded expenses are deducted	$	$	$
	$	$	$
TOTALS	$	$	$

"Middle age is a period of life when a man begins to feel friendly toward insurance agents."

It may be that we have $4,000 a year available for our first time-peg of our Super Second Life venture and that we are single or are paying all of our own expenses. We list our dreams, fill in the years when costs are incurred, and hope. If the total each year falls below $4,000, champion! Maybe there's room for even more or wilder dreams. (Note the first line on the form above. Couples or companions sharing expenses should complete the "Co-Funded Budget Sheet" first to determine any deductions that will limit the amount of personal dispensable funds they will have available when they calculate their "Personal Budget Sheets.")

But let's say that isn't the case. That in certain years our costs would be considerably above the amount, and below in other years. We're not without recourse. We might postpone an activity to a year with a surplus budget, or we might specifically or generally trim costs to squeeze everything in the desired years. Of course, we could simply save the money from the less demanding years and use it when the needs are greater. The fourth suggestion palls: we might do something (legal) to earn enough additional money in the short years to make the difference! (I won't suggest that again.)

The value of this form is that it allows us to get a mental grip on what we can do financially, and how we can trim sails or expand our views to fit a truly Super Second Life into our probably limited budget.

Personal Budget Sheets

Let's look at two sample, completed Personal Budget Sheets to get a sense of how they work and how budgets can be modulated to accommodate our desires. Expenses are calculated at a 2% inflation rate per annum. As you saw earlier, my wife and I had set a $10,000 annual discretionary funds limit apiece in the decade from 2001-2010.

PERSONAL BUDGET SHEET

Gordon Burgett / TIME-PEG (1): Years 2001-2010 / Date: xxx

Dreams:	2001	2002	2003
Funds available after co-funded expenses are deducted	$ 8,980	$8,959	$8,938
Phase out my C.U. publishing firm, probably between ages 65-70.	N.A.	N.A.	N.A.
Speak to associations, corporations, other groups about Super Second Life, 2-3 times a month until about 68 (or it isn't fun).	$2,500	$1,000	N.A.
Write a new book every two years, until about 68; including Perfect Human World book.	$250	N.A.	$250
Have 1.5-2 hours a day for uninterrupted reading.	N.A.	N.A.	N.A.
Play 18 holes of golf weekly with three other cronies.	$1,100	$1,122	$1,144
Travel annually to see my brothers, alternating them each year.	$997	$835	$997
Increase my activity with the local Barbershopper's group: weekly practice, perform with them when possible, attend a convention yearly, later join a quartet.	$800	$816	$832
Continue a steady exercise regimen at the local YMCA: run, cycle, or swim each once or twice a week (plus ab exercises, jacuzzi, and steam room after each session).	$150	$153	$156
Continue my Agemasters achievements as long as possible: cycle my age in miles (then kms); attempt to swim my age in kms; at 62 run my age in kms; add in age walk later.	$567	$578	$590
Maintain close contact with my wife's daughters and families.	$500	$510	$520
Maintain close contact with my sister and family.	$100	$102	$104
Perform in the *Messiah* 1-3 times annually at Christmas.	$25	$26	$26
Financially, maintain regular control over finances.	N.A.	N.A.	N.A.
TOTALS	$ 6,989	$ 5,142	$ 4,619

PERSONAL BUDGET SHEET
Marsha Freeman / TIME-PEG (1): Years 2001-2010 / Date: xxx

Dreams:	2001	2002	2003
Funds available after co-funded expenses are deducted	$8,980	$8,959	$8,938
Join forces with a leading consulting firm to sopify the dental world.	$1,200	N.A.	N.A.
Maintain my weight at 125-130 pounds.	N.A.	N.A.	N.A.
Be physically active through golf, walking, cycling, calisthenics, and sports.	$350	$357	$364
Visit my family in Tulsa and Arkansas four times a year.	$3,220	$3,284	$3,350
Interact with my children/grandchildren three to four times a week.	$300	$306	$312
Surround myself with warm, supportive, creative, positive-minded people.	N.A.	N.A.	N.A.
Read the daily paper and weekly/monthly periodicals.	$200	$204	$208
Create a college trust fund for my grandchildren.	$1,000	$1,000	$1,000
Buy a powerful laptop computer that will allow me to quickly access the Internet and to e-mail family and friends.	$2,000	N.A.	N.A.
Have a positive impact on everyone I meet.	N.A.	N.A.	N.A.
Become financially secure, wise, and responsible.	N.A.	N.A.	N.A.
Go on an annual retreat with women friends.	$1,000	$1,020	1,040
Write a how-to standard operating procedures book for the masses.	N.A.	$2,250	N.A.
Sightsee: visit historical sites, museums, art galleries, natural wonders.	$1,200	$1,224	$1,248
Be brave, courageous, disciplined, principled, and ethical, and live a life of integrity and honesty.	N.A.	N.A.	N.A.
TOTALS	$ 10,470	$ 9,645	$ 7,522

Can we do what we plan within our $10,000 annual discretionary budgets?

After deducting the co-funding expenses, I made it with room to spare but my wife fell short in the years 2001 and 2002, by $1,490 and $686.

If we were planning for 20 years hence, the numbers are close enough that we'd simply wait until the time came to make adjustments.

But our dates are nearly here! So she took a hard look at her dreams and quickly found two ways to reduce that $1,490 shortfall in 2001. Both require the same process: moving items from our personal to our business account. The first item, her joining forces with a leading consulting firm, should properly be an extension of the business sale, and come from those profits. And she decided that the small computer she now uses will be fine for her personal needs, and if her new employer provides a more powerful laptop for business, she can use it off hours for her needs as well. So that reduces the dream need total in 2001 from $10,470 to $7,270. The $1,710 surplus will be kept for the second year's use, more than canceling the $686 deficit in 2002.

We made it! If we hadn't, and there was difficulty deciding which dreams to limit (or other conflicts arose), the next chapter would help.

Co-Funded Budget Sheet

The second form is the "Co-Funded Budget Sheet," which covers those dreams which both members of an union mutually share, like trips or activities done together. The form looks almost identical except it is done for both at the same time and assumes, unless stipulated, that the expenses listed are shared equally. As mentioned earlier, *this form should be completed first*, if co-funding is an issue. Those shared expenses can be deducted from each person's individual spendable allotment.

An easy example: both mates have the same $4,000 to spend each year on dreams. They have one item only on their "Co-Funded Budget Sheet" and it is the same for all ten years: $2,000 annually for a trip to the sea. That means that each will spend $1,000 of their $4,000 that way, leaving $3,000 apiece for the items on their "Personal Budget Sheet."

The basis of how the money is allocated probably needs more explanation. It is that mates or companions usually operate one of two ways financially.

The first, and most common, is that their money comes from two sources. In it, their incomes are first pooled to pay for the basic needs such as shelter, food, health, insurance, transportation, and so on—the general living expenses—which also includes an emergency (or contingency) fund for such extraordinary things as health crises.

"Age doesn't matter unless you're a cheese."

Billie Burke

The secondary source is the discretionary, personal money that is left over, as surplus, after the pooled needs have been met. From that—as well as from other personal funds the person has already segregated (including the interest it earns) or from the stipulated earnings not pooled—they pay for their own dreams. Those latter funds are accounted for in the Personal Budget Sheet.

The second approach is that each person in the union pays their share of all expenses, and any money they do not pay is available to finance their dreams (or other, non-dream things). Those following this approach don't need a Co-Funded Budget Sheet.

Looking at our sample Co-Funded Budget Sheet, you must know that we had decided to split evenly all co-funded items each year. Thus the money left after calculating our halves of the joint dreams would be left for our individual (personal) dreams.

CO-FUNDED BUDGET SHEET Burgett-Freeman / TIME-PEG (1): Years 2001-2010 / Date: xxx			
Co-Funded Dreams:	2001	2002	2003
Have a warm, supportive, loving marriage.	N.A.	N.A.	N.A.
Sell the publishing company	N.A.	N.A.	N.A.
See two live plays or concerts per month	$1,200	$1,224	$1,249
Attend movies regularly (2.5 times a month)	$240	$245	$250
Visit my husband's daughters and family four times a year.	$600	$612	$624
TOTALS	$2,040	$2,081	$2,123

The first two aren't in the financial picture. True love is cheap. The second is in our business account, not personal, and will pay for itself through the sale. The third and fourth are simply items we enjoy together. The fifth requires a few hour's travel but they visit us as often as we do them so the costs are very modest. Missing are the usual large-priced expenses, like major travel. That is because we both still work and each travels extensively, sometimes together, so for this three-year period our additional travel will be individual and family-related, as you will see in our respective "Personal Fund Budget Sheets."

Assuming no changes, that means that we each must subtract $1020, $1041, and $1062 from our $10,000 allotment each year, leaving the remainder—$8980, $8959, and $8938—to be spent for personal dreams.

The beauty of all this is that we now have a detailed plan for the coming years, plus an action guide for each dream, starter steps, a look at any health considerations each carries, an indicator of what we might do now to prep to make the dream happen (or be more fun), and an indication of whether we will be able to afford the dreams. Soon we will see where we might store this valuable information.

Anything missing? Maybe. I'd suggest, for the more active and expensive dreams, an "Annual Action Record Sheet."

Annual Action Record Sheet

We're planning now for dreams to be filled in the near or distant future, with steps and cost estimates that may prove unreal when the actual time arrives. Some adjustments can be made on our budget sheets as the date draws closer, of course. But it makes sense to me to also keep an actual account of how the dreams work out, both in money and execution, while they are taking place, so that the ship can be better steered before it gets lost at sea.

If a form for that purpose would be helpful, this is how mine appears:

ANNUAL ACTION RECORD SHEET / Date:	
Dream:	**Year:**
Actions taken:	**Actual cost/income:**
Changes made this year:	**Changes suggested for the future:**

How might this help? Let me fictionalize a bit as if I were completing this form in 2002 and a family move had occurred. The budget that year called for $612 to be spent to visit my daughters, but that year it shot up to $1,150, which on a tight budget would mean that something would have to give.

You'll see in the completed Co-Funded Budget Sheet that follows that I'm now considering as a solution an annual family pow wow, at the Grand Canyon or at each other's homes, sometimes at Christmas. So this will require looking at some depth at both the Co-Funded Budget Sheet in 2003 and thereafter, plus checking the effect it will have on the dispensable cash for both of our Personal Budget Sheets. Plus it could impact Marsha's time with her family or daughters. Keeping an Annual Action Record Sheet forces me yearly to stay attuned to the Super Second Life plans and budget, to keep my dreams in sight and still realizable.

ANNUAL ACTION RECORD SHEET	
Dream: Visit my husband's daughters and family four times a year.	**Year: 2002**
Actions taken: Younger daughter and family moved to Albuquerque so we must reduce trips to once a year. Cost is about $400 higher.	**Actual cost/income:** $1,150
Changes made this year: Took one trip this year.	**Changes suggested for the future:** Am checking to see if whole family can meet at Grand Canyon in 2003 and annually at various homes in following years. Each family will take turns planning the gathering. May include Christmas every second or third year

Whether you want another form to complete or decide to simply adjust your future Budget Sheets at the end of each year (or on the "anniversary" date you chose to look at your Super Second Life plan—more in Chapter 17) is up to you.

Where can we keep our Final Action Plan, Money Worksheet, and Budget Sheets?

If you're like me, you have been experiencing a rising horror as the number of forms in this book keeps increasing. Not only does it imply more time spent completing forms than living your Super Second Life, it conjures up the certainty that the minute you finish creating your dream world, the papers will vanish and it will all be for naught!

Well, the forms are cumulative and if we've been keeping up, we simply had to add or modify an item per chapter, then enter them in the Final Action Plan. And if we put the results into our computer, it is all recoverable if, heavens, the paper gods or the vapors dematerialize our penned opus. (Copiers provide a similar back-up security.)

Where to put the final project? Let's not just hide it on the computer, where too often "out of sight is indeed out of mind."

While this is a serious and important project for us and our future, it's should also be a lot of fun. So let's make it as visible as we can.

Why not the easiest of physical storage formats? Buy one or several 2" brightly-colored three-ring binders and either use or print on three-holed paper (or hole punch it at the library or Kinkos). Less than $5 each. And if we print and post in huge letters—MY SUPER SECOND LIFE—on the outside of the binders, they will look sufficiently threatening and goofy to the unknowing that they will remain eternally untouched (by others).

The binder(s) will also have plenty of space for photos of our dreams being fulfilled, play programs, volunteer awards, and our Pulitzer notification. And they will be in sight at all time!

Of course, if we want to be daily inspired, we can reproduce our Final Action Plans in huge type and paste them wherever we regularly look. Further such inspiration, I defer to your genius.

Final Thoughts and a Paper Trail

Some final thoughts in defense of not only planning our Super Second Lives but keeping many of the details in written, accessible form.

The planning, and fulfillment, serves as a powerful model to others, particularly our children (and theirs). It shows us to be active, bright, forward-looking people who assume responsibility and control of our own lives. The kind of model that we would have respected and honored (and perhaps did) had we seen it carried through with such diligence and joy by our folks or others.

The records, including this final form, also provide a paper trail of our lives that can be read and hopefully admired by kin and others a hundred or a thousand years hence. If kept on a computer, they will be readily usable in some convertible format forever. What would we do today to have just such a record of our earlier ancestors?

That suggests other sections that we may wish to include in our binder, such as all the genealogical information we have (or can tap) about our family; a copy of our birth certificate and other official papers; photos of our family members and snapshots of our home(s) and prime possessions; perhaps our annual tax and health examination reports; all references (in the press), awards, and commendations; pertinent letters we wrote or received; even a personal recollection page summarizing the highlights of each year.

This might be done on a set date annually, like December 31 or after tax submission, in mid-April. How extensive or personal it becomes is, of course, up to each of us. But what a valuable historical and familial contribution that would be, particularly to those centuries hence who wouldn't have known what a crusty old eccentric we really are!

We're almost done. Conflict resolution, only if needed, is next. Then a few words about what we do next, and, in closing, some thoughts about periodic review, modification, and updating.

A Tool for Conflict Resolution Helps Reduce Resistance and Inertia

15

The first kind of conflict is evident: $500,000 worth of dreams and plans in a year with a $5,000 budget. It needn't be money. Conflicts can deal with time, energy, health, or a dozen other rubs. Or several of them at once. Without a tool to resolve such impasses now or when they occur, your Action Plan will quickly grind to a halt.

The second kind of conflict is more beguiling. You simply never get started. Not that you don't want to: you've made a sincere top-level commitment. You just haven't sufficiently analyzed all of the necessary action steps required to fulfill that commitment. Thus you haven't discovered the reasons why you can or will not comply, so you don't know how to offset them with solutions that will make that completion possible. Instead, you find yourself gripped by an inexplicable resistance or a paralyzing inertia. It makes your whole Action Plan seem like a cruel joke.

Two cures for the price of one! In this chapter you will learn a rather simple technique to both resolve conflicts and disarm resistance or inertia. Alas, you needn't wait until your later years to use it—it can be as easily applied to relationships or any other conflicts right now. It works at any time and for all ages!

Two potential hurdles scaled—and a lifetime technique learned!

In a perfect world...

In a perfect world we could do anything we wanted, without restraints. Our colleagues would cheer, God would smile, and the Nobel committee would stay in session trying to properly categorize our legion of achievements.

But in this world there's always some rub. Costs outrace dreams, *tempus fugit*, knees ache at three miles, and, damn it, we *are* going to die.

This chapter won't resolve the last, other than to help us fully fill the days (and nights) in between. But we can take a hard look at the rub, and give you a powerful tool to at least smooth it out, if not cure it.

There are conflicts, and then there are conflicts. Some are obvious: shouts, fists flying, sputum spat or biliously swallowed. And some aren't obvious: steps not taken, inaction driven by indecision, anger also eaten.

How does that affect our Super Second Life?

*The obvious
conflicts first*

These usually involve choices to be made. We have a tight June budget and three fun or noble opportunities that collectively require twice as much money as we have on hand. Or two events on the same day. Or having to program work, exercise, parents, gardening, a brake drum replacement, a bit part in the community theater play, and cheering on the neighbor in the yodeling semi-finals, most of it, it seems, simultaneously.

Solutions are equally as obvious. Flee to the cabin and mumble glumly about "the pains" reappearing. Or do things chronologically until we drop. Or stomp around bellowing about aliens or injustice ("If only...") until others ask us to quit. Most of us just nibble off what we want to chew, or must, or can't avoid. Ultimately, unpalatable solutions, if solutions at all.

*For more on this topic,
contact the William
Glasser Institute, 22024
Lassen St., Suite 118,
Chatsworth, CA 91311.
Phone (800) 899-0688;
website
www.wglasserinst.com*

Let me propose that conflicts be elevated to a different plain. (This thinking isn't original. You will find it much more fully developed by Drs. Robert Wubbolding and William Glasser in discussions about "Control Theory" and "Reality Theory." I'm merely applying the concept here to our Super Second Lives.)

It starts by asking "What do we really want?" Which is what we have already done when we created our Action Plans. Beyond those actions, it also asks the kind of person we want to be, which is the same as asking, as we did earlier, how we picture ourselves at a certain time—or now. Then it suggests that we become proactive in our decisions to make that picture come true or to make our actions that support that image a reality.

There are two worlds, the world we want and the present world as we perceive it. Rarely are they the same.

Using my own Action Plan, I may want to maintain close contact with my sister, her husband, and their son, but that's not happening, never has, and at the present rate probably never will.

Is there an exercise that will help resolve this dilemma?

Try making a list with three columns, the first labeled "What I want...," the second "The Gap of Resolution," and the third, "What I have."

CONFLICT RESOLUTION SHEET / Date:		
"What I want..."	"The Gap of Resolution"	"What I have..."

Then fill in the desire and the reality, leaving the middle blank.

CONFLICT RESOLUTION SHEET / Date:		
"What I want..."	"The Gap of Resolution"	"What I have..."
To maintain close contact with my sister, her husband, and son.		At present, virtually no contact except when I'm in the area.

The next step is to expand upon (or explain) the third column, as you perceive the difficulty at present. This is what comes to mind in my example:

1. They live about as far across the United States as one can go.
2. They are busy and thus difficult to communicate with.
3. We no longer share much in common.
4. They never visit our area.
5. I almost never visit their area.
6. We have no tradition of mutually honoring birthdays or even holidays.

It doesn't take a genius to see that, on the surface, none of these hinder my maintaining the close contact I desire. But in reality they do.

The gap between the world I want and what I perceive that I have—the "Gap of Resolution" above—is simply too great for me to enact my desires without some attention and, in this case, behavior modification. To cross the gap, that is what I must do.

I must switch to proactive, personal responses from my current reactive, external responses that simply keep things as they are to make the world that I want the world I get.

For example, if my sister would contact me, visit, live closer, stop being so busy and direct her attention my way, start sending Easter and Arbor Day cards, was on my wave length instead of setting the drama world aflame, or I was in her neighborhood regularly, none of this would be an issue. We'd permanently be in close contact. "If only" are the fatal words. Like she's the problem and I'm an innocent victim.

Of course it looks absurd in black and white. But that's the path to resolution, or at least understanding—putting it all down so that any objective eye, and heart, can gaze upon it for cloud-clearing clarification. Then changing my attitude and behavior to create what I want.

The hidden barriers

What hides in that "Gap of Resolution" are the behaviors that stop me from maintaining that close contact. And the emotional responses that obstruct or stimulate those behaviors, like anger, confusion, sense of abandonment, and frustration.

Rather than simply dwelling on those or analyzing them *ad nauseam*, I can simply ask, "What can I do to make what I want happen?" Rather than railing reactively and giving vent to those

*"Life is a play!
It's not its length,
but its performance
that counts."*

Seneca

emotions (and thus maintaining the status quo), what proactive steps can I take to bring us closer together and keep it that way?

Some things won't change. We will likely always live some distance apart, she will always be busy, and neither of us are likely to be physically near each other very often.

But there are things I can do.

1. I could call and explain that I'd like to keep in closer contact with her and her family now and in the future. (It's certain she has no idea that this is my current interest or intention.)
2. I could ask how we could do that, if she's in agreement that it's a good idea.
3. If she rejects the idea, or shrieks and slams down the phone, I will have to either reconsider my wishes or pursue this question in other ways.
4. If she is in agreement, implement her ideas, if they make sense and are doable.
5. Keep an e-mail contact alive every week or so.
6. Add an extra day or two to my trips near her home to visit at greater length, after checking to see if that's acceptable to her (and them).
7. Invite them to visit and stay with us in the future.
8. Stock up on Easter and Arbor Day cards....

This list may be half as long again after talking with her. The end result of my taking control, after identifying what isn't working now and what I'd like to have happen, would be both a clear line of communication and actual steps that I could take, plus an understanding of what I must do to keep this contact close and fresh.

***What about
overlapping dreams?***

But what if my wife and I had a future conflict that involved overlapping dreams? Would the same process or exercise help?

Say that she wanted to travel to Tulsa to see her folks, I was planning to run my age in kilometers (62, or 38.5 miles) and was counting on her logistical support, and both were taking place on, say, June 23. That is the date of her family's annual reunion and, by chance and for a whole series of odd reasons, the only possible date I can make the run that year. Neither are life-affecting actions but both are important to us.

In a perfect world, we would each fully support the other, me by at least applauding her attending the shindig (if not participating with her), she by helping man the drops during the run. But in the real world, we will be hundreds of miles apart.

Of course, one or the other could reschedule. But in our scenario that isn't possible. Instead, rather than creating some emotional impasse or anger, we simply list every problem that might occur that could prevent either of us from doing what we had planned, then work together proactively to solve them. If necessary, we could do this on separate Conflict Resolution Sheets, then share them to work out the solutions.

But that wouldn't be necessary for my wife since we both agree that it's fine for her to go, that I won't make it this time, and that there are no other problems in her case, like finances or health. All that's left, for her, is the doing.

On the other hand, I'm still left with a problem that could imperil my realizing my dream. That is, lack of logistical support. Thus:

CONFLICT RESOLUTION SHEET / Date:		
"What I want..."	"The Gap of Resolution"	"What I have..."
To run 62 kilometers on June 23.		No logistical support during the run.

> "Life is a fatal adventure. It can only have one end. So why not make it as far ranging and free as possible?"
>
> *Alexander Eliot*

If we set aside the fact that I'd like to share the accomplishment with her—there is little more heart warming than seeing your aging husband on some backwoods road gasping for air and stepping on his tongue—and we dismiss her certainty that I will drop dead at about 61.8 kilometers, we are left with the tough stuff, which prompts another list of my perception of difficulties in that third column from my achieving "what I want...":

1. I will need some defizzed Pepsi and water about every five miles, plus a banana at the second and an oatmeal cookie at the fourth location.
2. I'd like a shirt and headband change at about 20 miles.
3. If my running flats cause blisters, I'd like a second set of shoes available when needed.

4. I'd like to have somebody witness the start, finish, and that I completed the distance running.
5. I may need a sag wagon to bring me home if I don't make the full distance.

Alas, another "if only..." list that looks far less imposing on paper than when left undefined in the mind. In fact, it's embarrassingly clear that this can be done alone, since that was precisely how I ran 50 miles at 50. I'll simply modify the process:

1. I'll devise a double looped route that passes my house in the middle, at about 19.25 miles, so I will need hidden caches at about 5, 10, 15, 25, 30, and 35 miles—except that 5 and 25, 10 and 30, and 15 and 35 will be the same cache (requiring three instead of six) and they will only be 4.81 miles apart. All I did the first time was hide the plastic bottles and banana(s) inside a small box behind a tree or bush near the road, with a small red marker on the street to tell me where I should stop and hunt.
2. I can change clothes or even shower, if I wish, at the halfway spot at my house. And eat the cookie there.
3. I'll know by the time I get home after the first loop if I need to bandage my feet or change shoes.
4. Maybe I'll tell a neighbor, if it's still that important. I'll know I ran it!
5. A friend of mine will be home that day and I'll ask him if he'd pick me up if I called. There are at least five public phones along the route, so I'll carry 35 cents. Anyway, I won't be down long. The residents will spot the vultures and will surely call the police.

How does this help before-the-fact?

Usually there's a reason why folks don't just jump into realizing a dream, particularly when they've gone through all of the steps we have to put them down and spell them out. It's that they haven't thought through the negatives sufficiently well to have cleared an action path.

Let me use another example that was regularly suggested by participants as a future dream or goal at my "Super Second Life" workshops and is also one of my dreams: "I'd like to see a minimum of two live plays and concerts each month."

That seems straightforward enough, something that anyone can start immediately and extend into their dotage. But when I ask the workshop participants if they do that now, they all say no. "Why not?" yields the proof that makes my point.

They usually offer three reasons:

1. Their spouse or companion won't go with them.
2. They never know what is currently being performed.
3. It simply costs too much money.

In other words, they love the idea and want to do it for years to come but they had never really figured out why they aren't doing it now. Which prompts me to suggest that our system will work just as well for unrecognized conflicts, to clear the air to make our future dreams doable the moment we wish to begin: at 60, 71, or tomorrow.

Let's use the sheet once more, then look at solutions to each of these dream impediments after it.

CONFLICT RESOLUTION SHEET / Date:		
"What I want..."	"The Gap of Resolution"	"What I have..."
To attend two live plays or concerts each month.		Not doing so because of (1) no companionship, (2) no knowledge, and/or (3) no money.

1. Lots of options here: you simply go alone, you find another companion besides a spouse or a mate for one or both presentations each month, you join a theater or music club. Or you do some sleuthing as to why the companion says no. Is it the kind of play or concert? Is it the location, the hour, some hidden fear? Or is it their way or paying you back for not watching them play Senior Soccer? (Would watching an occasional soccer game win back a companion to the plays?)
2. Finding out what is being performed is as easy as checking the newspaper or the weekly throw-aways, getting on the theater mailing list, calling the theaters once a month, seeing if there's a local website listing, and having your friends keeping you informed.

3. Ever heard of ushering? You get a saved seat, have ushering companions, and it's absolutely free, if you'll gussy up a bit. Again, join theater senior groups, get a senior discount, see if they sell "rush" tickets at lower prices, go to the reduced-rate previews.

The problem is seldom finding the answers. Common sense, a few friends, and asking people knowledgeable about the topic will usually bring solid solutions. The problem is that we don't know what we don't know, and in this case it's those unthought of, hidden obstacles that prevent us from stepping right out and living our dreams even before their time.

"Life is either a daring adventure, or nothing."

Helen Keller

What we have shared is a simple tool that helps us brush away the unseen emotional cobwebs or creates an arena for discussion and problem solving—or both.

It's not a panacea but it works wonders by asking, quite simply, "What do we really want? What precisely is our dream? How do we want to be or act?" and then it asks, instead of that being so, "What is going on right now?"

The magic takes place when we list our reactive perception, then find and take the proactive steps that can make our dream come true.

"Have you ever thought how solemn a thing it is to live? If you are grateful for your life, set a value on it: find out how much it is worth, and if it falls below what you would have it, begin to increase its value. ... be full of hope and love, and resolve to make as much of life as you can."

Ida Scott Taylor

What Do You Do Now? | 16

Here you are, the only person on your block who knows how to create your own Action Plan to spiff up your extra 30 years. But it's still just so many words and a rolling avalanche of funny sounding forms, each a reason for abandoning the whole thing and just quietly getting old without interference or interruption!

Don't quit! You simply need an annotated checklist to help you put the words into motion! Amuse and amaze your friends by your cleverness and energy!

What is the first decisive action you take to spank life into your newborn baby?

And how do you get used to referring to and carrying out an Action Plan after 40 or 50 years of living by (or on) the seat of your pants?

Old dog and new tricks. Alas, we all learn the tricks that we want to learn. That's the clue.

A checklist to put the Action Plan together.

A checklist

First of all, congratulations! You've read this far—a high sign that you may, in fact, convert yourself into a bona fide Super Second Lifer, with action plans, time-pegs, and great expectations for a fun 30 extra years or more.

The thinking, deciding, prioritizing, planning, and putting all that down on paper doesn't just happen. It's done by winners!

Even if you baled out a couple of times—a huge bonus if you read this straight through!—you've reached the finish line (almost). Now it's time to channel your excitement into a finished product.

What are the most important things that you must do to make this process work? Prepare a Dream List, then create an Action Plan. Those are the heart, the legs, and the fun. Capturing fantasy, writing yourself in, then pulling it off.

So I'd slip off, without distractions or time restraints, and let my imagination wander. Don't worry if brilliance isn't instant. Start with what you're doing now that you'd like to do forever. Add in the things you can't (or don't) do now but ring a happy bell. Include activities you see others doing that you admire and want to try. Forget the costs or even health concerns: those can usually be bent around a solid dream. And forget special skills or training that you think they have or you might need. Far more powerful is your desire.

When you run out of initial ideas or dreams, think in age boxes. We usually plan first for the 55-65 year period. Think of boxes for the successive decades: what would you also like to be doing then? What do you see others in that age group doing that you'd like to try? And what can you do from 40-55 that will make the later dreams easier and more fun?

Now we bring all the work together

What about all those other charts and boxes in this book? They make it easier to develop your Dream List and create your Action Plan. They are helpful stepping stones that lead you through the process of converting dreams and supercharging your last years.

Let's put each of those stepping stones into a check-off chart, with a quick explanation of how they fit into the Super Second Life process:

SUPER SECOND LIFE PROCESS CHECK-OFF CHART			
Chapter / Item		**Explanation**	**Done!**
2	Me Now List #1	The five lists help us see what we've done and learned, who we are now, and what we want to do later. A quick look at ourselves. They help pave the way to creating a more comprehensive and realistic Dream List.	
2	Me Now List #2		
2	Me Now List #3		
2	Me Now List #4		
2	Me Now List #5		
4	Super Second Life "In" List	What do we want to keep and/or build from in our later days?	
4	Super Second Life "Out" List	What do we want excluded from those later days?	
6	Medical Health History Questionnaire	A good look at our personal and family health, to factor into our coming and future plans.	
7	Super Second Life Net Worth Worksheet	Shows what we are worth now and may be at key points in our future. Hard to plan not knowing this.	
7	Super Second Life Income Worksheet	What we earn and gather now, and how we can change this when we wish in the future.	
7	Super Second Life Expense Worksheet	Where our money goes now, and may in the future. Shows where we can better economize when needed.	
7	Super Second Life Money Worksheet	The critical summary sheet. Can be updated at any point in the future. Needed for the Action Plan.	
8	Super Second Life Dream List	Without dreams, or direction, it's hard to plan a vital, fun, worthwhile future. The Action Plan starts here.	
9	Time-Pegs	Lists dreams by age, to match them with the ability, energy, and wherewithal to make them happen.	
10	Commitment	We grade dreams by our commitment to live them, focusing only on the most wanted.	
11	Personal Dream List	If coupled, this lets us separate our personal dreams from the overlapping or shared dreams.	
11	Overlapping or Shared Dream List	Lets us identify the dreams that we, as a couple, want to share together.	
12	Action Step Worksheet	First step in creating an Action Plan. Here we define what steps are required to put the dream in action.	
13	Action Step Worksheet	Expanded to add the costs and potential income of each dream.	
13	Joined Action Step Worksheet	An Action Step Worksheet for two!	
14	Final Action Plan	One per dream, these are the core of creating our own Super Second Lives. Time-pegged, they include the dream, cost, action steps, financial calculations, health considerations, and preparatory actions.	

14	Personal Budget Sheet	Brings all the dreams together in one time-peg to see what can be afforded and accomplished when.	
14	Co-Funded Budget Sheet	A Personal Budget Sheet for two, to help identify the joined funds, usually spent first.	
14	Annual Action Record Sheet	Helps us keep track of the dream's development over many years, by keeping an annual update.	

Let others help

"Life was meant to be lived, and curiosity must be kept alive. One must never, for whatever reason, turn his back on life."

Eleanor Roosevelt

There might be another box to check: Are you sharing everything about your projected Super Second Life with anybody who cares? Ask them questions, seek their advice, let them help you form your plans—remembering that, in the end, those dreams must be authentically yours to create your own best life.

Why not do at least part of the project with a friend, or another couple, or even a group of friends from the same age bracket? Why row into the future alone? I'm constantly amazed at the synergy that takes place in my Super Second Life workshops: the energy that is created and the excellent ideas we wouldn't have known had we not been on the same quest.

The same with solutions to pesky, even strange, problems. The least likely person digs into their peculiar well of experience or the stories they've heard, and suddenly a novel answer to a knotty problem emerges.

The truth is, a bunch of us are going to grow old together, whether we want to or not. For part of our journey, why not tramp through the same forest with similarly aging compadres, if for no other reason than for the companionship? And why not map the path now, even though the trek for meaning, purpose, and fun is still a while off?

You can brag too

You have permission to brag about having laid out a plan with specific purposes for your own future. Just by doing that you have risen to the top of the ranks. You are proactively taking control of your life and doing precisely what you want to do, after decades of fulfilling your role as student, spouse, worker, parent, and community helper. You don't stop being the others, but in the second half of your life they become part of your larger design. They are choices you make, among many choices. They are vibrant threads in an exciting fabric that you—*you*—are measuring, dyeing, weaving, and wearing.

They are but part of a life where you have an understanding and control of your finances. Where you have finally assumed responsibility for your health, and built a life pattern that finds you using your body, mind, energy, and hopes as you wish to use them.

More than brag, post your dream sheets, in final Action Plan form, where at least you can see them daily, to remind you of that thread, that fabric, that is letting you live as fully and with as much direction and vigor as humanly possible. The alternative—just bouncing along, really out of control, reacting rather than planning, filling in your days with no real direction or purpose—is unthinkable.

You're a winner!

Brag good and loud. You're a Super Second Lifer. You're a winner!

"Retirement is not the closing of an old door, but the opening of a new one. It is the exciting approach to an infinite variety of new testing of a man's ability, new stretchings of his mind, new releases for his energies and abilities. All that is required is that he must recognize new challenge when it presents itself, and accept it zestfully. If he has been doing this all of his life, it will be easier for him in the later years, but in one form or another the opportunity awaits everyone, if he will only seek it."

Clarence Randall

An Action Plan Needs Periodic Review, Modification, and Updating

17

We're almost done.

In today's world, nothing is permanent—except change. So you can expect that even the spiffiest turbojet Super Second Life Action Plan will need periodic review, modification, and updating. If for no other reason than the person writing the first version at 40 or 50 will only faintly resemble the person living it out at 70 or 90.

What looks reasonable yet challenging in the first draft might look stodgy and stale to a tripper of the light fantastic several decades hence. Or exhausting to a person whose new later-life loves are Toltecan novels and lawn bowling.

Fifteen years ago who could have thought of learning how to use a home computer so you could surf the Internet or create your own interactive website? Who knows what newfangled things will delight you fifteen years from now, much less 30?

So this chapter suggests reviewing your Action Plan, sprucing it up, trimming it back, or pointing it in some new direction. It suggests specific times when that might be done, even rewards for you not only being the brightest person on the block but for being brighter yet by keeping your Action Plan and you current.

If you're to be up-to-date, keep your Action Plan current. Here's how.

If we'll change in 30 years, so will our plan

Anybody wise enough to create their own Super Second Life knows that it's an ongoing labor of love. Nothing built around a dynamic existence is ever quite done!

On these pages we talk about 30 or more years of a super life. Thirty years is the time, in reverse, that it took you to have kids and settle in a job, get married, finish your education, raise hell in high school (or wish you had!), play ball, steal your first kiss, get lost in the museum on a school trip, memorize all 50 (or 48) states, learn to ride a bike and swim, take your first school bus ride, play with your brothers and sisters, and be your parents' fat-cheeked, gurgling pride!

Look at the astounding number of changes that took place during that time!

It's no different in the second half of our lives than it was in the first, except that now we can control many of the changes and appropriately respond to the rest.

Thus an Action Plan carefully put together at 45 or 50 will still provide us with a path and a direction at 65 or 80, even though the background and the tools, means, and maybe even the determination may be dramatically different.

In our Action Plan dreaming we started with mental images of how we wanted to be at certain points in our life. Now we must ask, are we fulfilling those dreams, despite, or perhaps because of, the changes? And what must we review, and perhaps modify or update, to bring us and those visions into a brighter, truer focus?

If a Super Second Life plan needs periodic adjustments, is it a waste of time to lay it out now? No more than it is to map out a trip days, months, or even a year in advance. The trip is the point, not whether the road is subsequently renumbered, a motel along the way has changed its name, or when we travel we change our plan en route.

It's also much easier, with the trip on the calendar and the excitement generated, to modify the details. If we're still eager to take the trip, then leaving a day or a week earlier, driving in a van rather than a coupe, and zigging past Uncle Elmo's en route are simply wrinkles of an already exciting cloth.

The alternative? What usually happens when we have no plan is nothing. It's the same in travel or life.

What Are You Going to Do With Your Extra 30 Years?

One day a year...

"The advantage of being eighty years old is that one has had many people to love."

Jean Renoir

Dream update!

The smartest thing is to set aside part of one day each year to review our entire Super Second Life program. To get out our sheets or call up the file on our computer and give it a thorough, detailed going over.

Whether alone, with a companion, or with some close friends who care, it's worth an hour, or several, to see what we've accomplished, what is pending, and how we are faring on our lifetime venture. A reward should accompany that doing too: a special meal, some festive outing, or our annual bath.

Why not use our birthday as the chosen date? Or some special anniversary? Some date that won't slip by unnoticed.

That's also a particularly good time to review our financial situation, gathering whatever data needed to create a current status sheet to compare with the others from previous years. Then if adjustments need be made, the week or ten days following might be dedicated to righting our ship.

No less important is our health, so that might be the day to schedule our annual check-up—or whatever a knowledgeable, wise bill of health requires.

It's good to stop at set intervals to see precisely how we are faring now compared to this time last year. Let's admit it: we're all going to die. But are we getting there as slowly, gracefully, and joyfully as we can? As much as possible, are we in control of our own destiny, or at least the stops along the way? Are we eking out of every moment what we want and need, without preventing or impeding others from doing the same?

Review time is a chance to reread our Dream Lists. Are some of those lesser dreams that never hit the action level starting to look particularly appealing? Are you dabbling in something new that might be worth a new Action Plan and some dedicated implementation? Is it time to put some fire under a listed, top-priority dream that just sits there—or is this the day to dump it, as an idea whose time never really came?

Are we using our money wisely? Is it time to shift financial allocations? If you're planning to leave funds to your children or others, is it time to think about starting that now, within the tax-free annual gift limitations, so they can use it to plan their Super Second Lives—or enrich their early years?

185

By now you understand the process. There's no magic to updating, nor any reason to go through the steps, other than to suggest that deletions and additions to Action Plans at any time are as natural and welcome as new names on a family roster and old addresses penned out and corrected in your address books.

Our lives are at stake here. Without asking, we've been given a gift of 30 extra years. It's up to us to figure out what we're going to do with that gift. Ignoring it seems, at least, ungrateful. And with a plan, we can extract many more drops of delight and share many more touches of love.

So these pages propose that each of us figure out the ways to make our dreams come true in those extra 30 years—and by keeping our plan consistently renewed, add new dreams and refresh and expand old ones.

Congratulations too

My wish to you is that every one of your second-life dreams comes true.

APPENDIX: CONTENTS

```
200 MORE IDEAS
FOR A
SUPER SECOND LIFE
```

There are literally thousands of worthwhile, exciting things to do during our Super Second Lives, and many of lesser eminence. Here are 200 suggestions, to add to the 32 in Chapter 8. (If you wish to share your best ideas, please e-mail them to **dreamlist@agemasters.com** *and we will post them at* **www.agemasters.com** *under "Dream List" for your enjoyment.)*

act as a liaison for a CARE "Adopt a School" Program

adopt a pet

assist at a homeless shelter

assist the choir director or pianist/organist at church

be a site facilitator for the Special Olympics

be the radio-TV liaison for non-profit groups

become a baseball umpire

become a clown

become a commissioned fingerprint specialist

become a court watcher

become a crossing guard

become a history docent of the town for the schools

become a legal assistant specialist

become a liaison between senior groups and local educational programs

become a lifeguard

become a local charity fund-raiser

become a mime

become a notary public

become a private investigator

become a swimming/diving instructor

become a visiting school "grandma" or "grandpa"

become an ombunsdperson for the library, city, or local services

become an oral historian for city archives

become an usher: theater, concerts, sports events

become proficient at wine tasting

become the city site photographer for historical preservation

can food and share it with others in need

catalog the local flora and/or fauna

chaperone kids or pre-teens to museums

chaperone kids or pre-teens to sports events

chaperone youth on church missionary programs

coach for youth leagues

compete in senior Olympics programs

convert your family photos to digital

create a family newsletter

create a guide to city or county festivals or activities

create a guide to city or county recreational facilities

create a local cycling map

create a map of city or county beauty routes (with mile markers)

create a map of city or county bridal paths (with mile markers)

create a map of city or county hiking paths (with mile markers)

create a map of city or county running paths (with mile markers)

create a paid proofreading service

create a website for your city or library

create a written family genealogy

create an historical guide to city or county buildings and sites

What Are You Going to Do With Your Extra 30 Years?

create an historical guide to past city or county
   festivals or activities
create and hold a treasure hunt for your family
   or local groups
create computer support for city and county
   boards or groups
create your own website
cycle your age (miles or kilometers)
deliver meals to shut-ins (Meals on Wheels
   programs)
develop a home medical transcription service
direct the church choir
do extra-hand work for your church, like
   painting and carpentering
drive a bus for a local transport company
drive the school bus
fix old bicycles to donate to youth programs
focus on and effectuate one specific act of city
   beautification
form a musical group: band, quartet, etc.
form a senior writer's group
gather crop surpluses for use at welfare feeding
   programs
gather used instruments for schools or youth
   groups
get and care for a horse
handle public relations for non-profit groups
help at day care during church services
help at local swim meets (records/timing)
help at local track meets (records/timing)
help at local youth league competitions
   (records/timing, etc.)
help at other local athletic events, like
   triathlons, marathons, runs
help candidates running for office
help design and plant a city flower bed
help prepare meals for welfare programs
help seniors install their computers
help supervise playground and school recess
help teach a foreign language at school
help the Braille Institute
help the poor or elderly file legal papers
help the poor or elderly prepare tax forms
help transfer written records to digital form
help your minister with home visitations

host a senior's radio/TV program
join a barbershop quartet
join a drumming group
learn a new trade
learn and master Aikido
learn and master belly dancing
learn and master calligraphy
learn and master handwriting analysis
learn and master line dancing
learn and master listening
learn and master meditation
learn and master papermaking
learn and master T'ai Chi
learn and master yoga
learn and practice sustainable gardening
learn and practice time management
learn bookkeeping and offer your skills to non-
   profit groups
learn estate planning
learn fresh water kayaking
learn landscape drawing
learn Latin dance, like Salsa and Merengue
learn or play a musical instrument
learn photography
learn self-defense
learn self-hypnosis / autosuggestion
learn to build instruments
learn to build your own stock portfolio
learn to converse with your spouse
learn to knit
learn to paint
learn to play the guitar
learn to produce booklets to share your family
   writings with kin/local library
learn to put folk songs to a musical score
learn to repair household appliances
learn to repair instruments
learn to sculpt
learn to sell your writing to magazines and
   newspapers
learn to serve as a group facilitator
learn to throw and glaze pottery
learn to weave
learn to write grant proposals
learn vegetarian soapmaking

189

What Are You Going to Do With Your Extra 30 Years?

maintain an updated list of local child care
  programs

maintain an updated list of local youth programs

manage small rental properties

offer free proofreading for student writers

officiate at local youth leagues

organize a church singles program

organize a master family photo album

organize an investment club

organize church senior drama and music
  programs

organize the records or archives for a local
  group

participate in city site preservation programs

perfect your ballroom dancing

provide holding care for infants at a hospital or
  orphanage

provide library pick-up/delivery service for
  folks in hospital or care homes

quit smoking

read aloud to children at the school or library

research/write travel articles for/about the aged,
  challenged, women alone

run for city, township, county, state, or national
  office

sell your photos to magazines and newspapers

sew a family quilt

stack books in the library

take the elderly, children, or newcomers to the
  library

teach basic computer skills to seniors

teach children how to churn butter and ice
  cream

teach children to bake

teach children to knit

teach children to weave

teach devotional studies classes

teach do-it-yourself car repair

teach do-it-yourself home repair

teach do-it-yourself landscaping

teach English in an ESL program

teach inheritance management

teach job application skills

teach kids how to repair bicycles

teach or help at vacation Bible school

teach others how to can (or preserve) food

teach others how to create their website

teach photography to kids or seniors

teach reading in a literacy program

teach self-defense to seniors

teach Sunday School

train others to record local records or sites for
  the city or library

visit retirement or convalescent homes

volunteer for medical tests/questionnaires

volunteer for the Special Olympics

volunteer to help at a men's center

volunteer to help at a women's center

volunteer to help on school field trips

walk students to/from school

walk your age (miles or kilometers)

work as a dental or medical office receptionist

work at the polls

work on city, county, or regional beautification

write a column for the local newspaper

write a family history

write a novel

write a senior's column for the newspaper

write a syndicated column

write a TV script

write and sell greeting cards

write book reviews for newspapers and
  magazines

write grant proposals for non-profit groups

write how-to articles

write lyrics

write movie reviews for newspapers and
  magazines

write music

write poetry

write the history book of your town or county

write the history of your family's cars/vehicles

write the history of your family's homes

write the history of your family's pets

write the history of your family's vacations

write travel articles

write/publish about local artists and writers

write/publish about local historical events and
  sites

write/publish about local prehistory

teach math jr high

Kit Car
Build Home

190

LOCAL RESOURCES

Almost every county or region in the U.S. has a guide to local non-profit agencies and resources. And most of these, it seems, are directed to or help folks 40+. Your reference librarian will lead you to your community resources directory.

For example, in my county there is the ***Santa Barbara County's Comprehensive Guide to Public and Private Non-Profit Human Resources***. Listed in the SENIORS category are care management, seniors centers, in-house care, legal, legislation, low income (free meals, cottages, housing corporations), employment, out-of-house care, programs, psychiatric help, recreation, transportation, adult education, lawn bowling, parks and recreation programs, dancing, volunteering, nutrition sites, and the YMCA.

But it doesn't stop there because in the hundreds of additional listings are A.A., Alzheimer's, arts and crafts, assisted living, blood pressure, senior board and care, care-giving, clinics, clubs and organizations, barbershop groups, cards, congregate meals, and computer teaching and assistance.

If you want to contact national groups, to commune with other souls with interests as bizarre as your own, check your library's current edition of the ***Encyclopedia of Associations***. It lists groups dedicated to almost anything. A few listings: Shoplifters Anonymous, Museum Volunteers, Hearing Dog Project, and the Cage Bird Judging Association.

Want to travel, meet others your age, and not spend a fortune? Than write the ***Elderhostel*** at 75 Federal Street, Boston, MA 02110 and request a copy of their huge, thick quarterly catalog: it features US and Canadian programs for three of the quarters, international travel each fall. About 2,000 colleges or institutions take part. If you're 55+, for about $350-450 a week (fees, board, room, and classes) you can learn almost anything anywhere, like opera, jazz, the Kentucky Derby, photography, trekking, skiing, pottery, or the history of Black Hawk.

The best local resources? Start at the library, then the City Hall, Chamber of Commerce, the local recreation program, and your church. Ask each to suggest additional resources. You'll be amazed, as I was, at the bounty physically within reach or immediately accessible by mail, phone, e-mail, or the Internet. (No computer? Use the library's.)

GENERAL ORGANIZATIONS:

RESOURCE LIST
for
SUPER SECOND LIFERS

In the three resource categories that follow—general, health, and finances—I am including associations or organizations with services of interest to those 40+. Where available, the listing includes the name of the group, address, phone, and website address (after http://www.) *You can also download a link to all website references in this book at www.agemasters.com.*

Administration on Aging, Eldercare Locator, 330 Independence Avenue SW, Room 4656, Washington, DC 20201 / (202) 619-0724 / nih.gov

American Association of Homes and Services for the Aging, 901E St. NW, Suite 500, Washington, DC 20004-2011 / (202) 783-2242 / aahsa.org

American Association of Retired Persons (AARP), 601 E St. NW, Washington, DC 20049 / (202) 434-2277

American Geriatrics Society, 770 Lexington Ave., Suite 300, New York, NY 10021 / (212) 308-1414 / americangeriatrics.org

American Public Human Services Association, 810 First St. NE, Suite 500, Washington, DC / (202) 682-0100 / aphsa.org

American Red Cross, 1621 N. Kent St., 11th Floor, Arlington, VA 22209 / (703)248-4222 / redcross.org

American Society on Aging, 833 Market St., Suite 511, San Francisco, CA 94103 / (415) 474-9600

Disabled American Veterans, 3725 Alexandria Pike, Cold Spring, KY 41076 / (606) 441-7300 / dav.org

National Aging Resource Center on Elder Abuse, 1010 Wayne Avenue, Suite 800, Silver Springs, MD 20910-5633 / (301) 562-2400

National Association for Hispanic Elderly, 1452 W. Temple St., Suite 100, Los Angeles, CA 90026-1724

National Association for Home Care, 228 7th St. SE, Washington, DC 20003 / (202) 547-7424 / nahe.org

National Association of Area Agencies on Aging, 1112 16th St. NW, # 100, Washington, DC 20036-4823 / (202) 296-8130 / ncoa.org/naaaa.htm

National Caucus and Center on Black Aged, Inc., 1424 K St. NW, Suite 500, Washington, DC 20005 / (202) 637-8400

General Organizations: Resource List for Super Second Lifers (2)

National Council on the Aging, Inc., 409 Third St. NW, Washington, DC 20024 / (202) 479-1200 / ncoa.org

National Council on Patient Information and Education, 666 11th Street NW, Suite 810, Washington, DC 20001 / nap.edu

National Council on Senior Citizens, 8403 Colesville Rd., Suite 1200, Silver Spring, MD 20910-3314 / (301) 578-8800 / ncscinc.org

National Council on the Aging, 409 Third St. SW, Washington, DC 20024 / (202) 479-1200 / ncoa.org

National Hospice Organization, 1901 North Moore St., Suite 901, Arlington, VA 22209-1714 / (703) 243-5900 / nho.org

National Institute of Aging Information Center, P.O. Box 8057, Gaithersburg, MD 20857 / (800) 222-2225 / nih.gov

United Seniors Health Cooperative, 409 Third St. SW, Second Floor, Washington, DC 20024 / (202) 479-6973 / ushc-online.org

> ## HEALTH ORGANIZATIONS:
>
> RESOURCE LIST
> for
> SUPER SECOND LIFERS

Alzheimer's Association, 919 North Michigan, Suite 1000, Chicago, IL 60611 / (800) 272-3900 / alz.org

American Academy of Dermatology, 930 N. Meacham Rd., Schaumberg, IL 60173-4965 / (847) 330-0230 / derm.infonet.com

American Academy of Facial Plastic and Reconstructive Surgery, 310 S. Henry St., Alexandria, VA 22314-3524 / (703) 299-9291

American Academy of Neurology, 1080 Montreal Ave., St. Paul, MN 55116-2325 / (651) 695-1940

American Academy of Ophthalmology, PO Box 7424, San Francisco, CA 94120-7424 / (415) 561-8500 / eyenet.org

American Academy of Orthopedic Surgeons, 6300 North River Rd., Rosemont, IL 60018-4262 / (847) 823-7186 / aaos.org

American Academy of Otolaryngology—Head and Neck Surgery Inc., One Prince St., Alexandria, VA 22314-3357 / (703) 836-4444 / entnet.org

American Association of Cardiovascular and Pulmonary Rehabilitation, 7611 Elmwood Ave., Suite 201, Middleton, WI 53562 / (608) 831-6989 / aacvpr.org

American Cancer Society Inc., National Headquarters, 1599 Clifton Rd. NE, Atlanta, GA 30329 / (800) 227-2345 / cancer.org

American College of Obstetricians and Gynecologists, 409 12th St. SW, Washington, DC 20024-2188 / (202) 638-5577 / acog.org

American Dental Association, 211 E. Chicago Avenue, Chicago, IL 60611 / (312) 440-7494 / ada.org

American Diabetes Association, 1660 Duke St., Alexandria, VA 22314-3447 / (800) 342-2383 / diabetes.org

American Foundation for the Blind, 11 Penn Plaza, Suite 300, New York, NY 10001 / (800) AFB-LINE / afb.org

American Heart Association, 7272 Greenville Ave., Dallas, TX 75231-4596 / (800) 242-1793 / americanheart.org

American Liver Foundation, 1425 Pomptom Ave., Cedar Grove, NJ 07009 / (800) GO-LIVER / sadieu.ucsf.edu/alf/alfFinal

American Lung Association, 1740 Broadway, 14th Floor, New York, NY 10019-4374 / (212) 315-8700 / lingusa.org

Health Organizations: Resource List for Super Second Lifers (2)

American Optometric Association, 243 North Lindbergh Blvd., St. Louis, MO 63141-7881 / (800) 365-2219 / aoanet.org

American Parkinson's Disease Association, 1250 Hylan Blvd., Suite 4B, Staten Island, NY 10305 / (800) 223-2732

American Podiatric Medical Assoc., 9312 Old Georgetown Rd., Bethesda, MD 20814-1698 / (301) 571-9200 / apma.org

American Tinnitus Association, PO Box 5, Portland, OR 97207-0005 / (800) 634-8978 / ata.org

Arthritis Foundation, 1330 Peachtree St., Atlanta, GA 30309 / (800) 283-7800

Cancer Information Service, NIC/HIH, Bldg. 31 10A07, 31 Center Drive, MSC 2580, Bethesda, MD 20892-2580 / (800) 4-CANCER

Epilepsy Foundation, 4351 Garden City Dr., Landover, MD 20785 / (800) 332-1000 / efa.org

Glaucoma Research Foundation, 490 Post St., Suite 830, San Francisco, CA 94102 / (800) 826-6693 / glaucoma.org

Huntington's Disease Society of America, 140 West 22d St., 6th Floor, New York, NY 10011-2420 / (800) 345-4372 / hdsa.com

International Hearing Society, 20361 Middlebelt Rd., Livonia, MI 48152 / (800) 521-5247 / hearingins.org

Lupus Foundation of America, 1300 Piccard Dr., Suite 200, Rockville, MD 20850 / (800) 558-0121 / lupus.org

National Alliance for the Mentally Ill, 200 N. Glebe Rd., Suite 1015, Arlington, VA 22203-3754 / (703) 524-7600 / nami.org

National Arthritis and Musculoskeletal and Skin Diseases Information Clearing House, 1 AMS Circle, Bethesda, MD 20892-2350 / (301) 495-4484 / nih.gov/niams

National Digestive Diseases Information Clearinghouse, 2 Information Way, Bethesda, MD 20892-3507 / niddk.nih.gov/health/digest/nddic.htm

National Eye Institute, 2020 Vision Place, Bethesda, MD 20892-3655 / (301) 496-5248

National Headache Foundation, 428 W. St. James Place, 2nd Floor, Chicago, IL 60614-2750 / (800) 843-2256 / headaches.org

National Institute of Neurological Disorders and Stroke, P.O. Box 5801, Bethesda, MD 20824 / nih.gov

National Institute on Deafness and Other Communication Disorders, NIH, 31 Center Drive, MSC 2320, Bethesda, MD 20892-2320 / (301) 496-7243 / nih.gov/nidcd

National Kidney and Urologic Diseases Information Clearinghouse, 3 Information Way, Bethesda, MD 20892-3560 / (301) 654-4415 / niddk.nih.gov

National Kidney Foundation, 30 East 33d St., 11th Floor, New York, NY 10016 / (800) 622-9010 / kidney.org

National Mental Health Association, Information Center, 1021 Prince St., Alexandria, VA 22314-2971 / nmha.org

Health Organizations: Resource List for Super Second Lifers (3)

National Osteoporosis Foundation, 1232 22nd St. NW, Washington, DC 20037-1292 / (202) 223-2226 / nof.org

National Society to Prevent Blindness, 500 East Remington Rd., Schaumberg, IL 60173-4557 / (800) 331-2020 / preventblindness.org

Self Help for Hard of Hearing People, 7910 Woodmont Ave., Suite 1200, Bethesda, MD 20814 / (301) 657-2249 / shhh.org

Skin Cancer Foundation, 245 5th. Avenue, Suite 1403, New York, NY 10156 / (800) SKIN-490 / skincancer.org

The Simon Foundation for Continence, PO Box 815, Wilmette, IL 60091 / (800) 23-SIMON

United Ostomy Association, 19772 MacArthur Blvd #200, Irvine, CA 92612-2405 / (800) 826-0826 / voa.org

United Parkinson's Foundation, 833 West Washington Blvd., Chicago, IL 60607 / (312) 733-1893

FINANCIAL / INVESTMENT ORGANIZATIONS:

RESOURCE LIST
for
SUPER SECOND LIFERS

American Association of Individual Investors, 625 N. Michigan Avenue, Suite 1900, Chicago IL 60611-3110 / (312) 280-0170

Association of Jewish Aging Services, 316 Pennsylvania Avenue SE, Suite 402, Washington, DC 20003-1175 / (202) 543-7500

Association of Private Pension and Welfare Plans, 1212 New York Avenue NW, Suite 1250, Washington, DC 20005-3987 (202) 289-6700 / appwp.org

Institute of Certified Financial Planners, 3801 E. Florida Avenue, Suite 708, Denver, CO 80210-2571 / (303) 2571

International Association for Financial Planners, 5775 Glenridge Dr. NE, #B-300, Atlanta, GA 30328-5364 / (800) 945-4237 / iafg.org

National Association of Health Plans, 1129 20th St. NW, Suite 600, Washington, DC 20036-3403 / (202) 778-3200 / aahp.org

National Association of Personal Financial Advisors, 355 W. Dundee Road, Suite 200, Buffalo Grove, IL 60089-3500 / (847) 537-7722 / napfa.org

National Organization of Social Security Claimants Representatives, 6 Prospect St., Midland Park, NJ 07432-1634 / (201) 444-1415 / nosscr.org

ME NOW LIST #1 / Date:			
Contributions Achievements Activities	Skills Developed	Ways I used these skills in my first life	Ways I might apply these skills in my second life

(See Chapter 2 for more information about how this list is used.)

ME NOW LIST #2 / Date:		
An objective person would use these adjectives to describe me now	Adjectives no longer applicable that they might have used about me in my first life	New adjectives I would like them to properly use about me during my second life

(See Chapter 2 for more information about how this list is used.)

ME NOW LIST #3 / Date:	I'm putting an "X" by those that I want to continue to describe my second life
These 10 words describe my first life:	
1.	
2.	
3.	
4.	
5.	
6.	
7.	
8.	
9.	
10.	

(See Chapter 2 for more information about how this list is used.)

If this is a library book or is available for multiple or public use, do <u>not</u> write on this form. Please copy it first and write on your copy! Thank you.

ME NOW LIST #4 / Date:		
These are attitudes, activities, traits, etc. that I want to leave at the gate	These are strengths I now possess that I want to take into my second life	These are strengths I want to develop in my second life

(See Chapter 2 for more information about how this list is used.)

ME NOW LIST #5 / Date:
These 10 words would add joy and worth to my "Super Second Life"
1.
2.
3.
4.
5.
6.
7.
8.
9.
10.

(See Chapter 2 for more information about how this list is used.)

SUPER SECOND LIFE "IN" LIST

What you want to include in your Super Second Life

Date:

1.	
2.	
3.	
4.	
5.	
6.	
7.	
8.	
9.	
10.	
11.	
12.	
13.	
14.	
15.	
16.	
17.	
18.	
19.	
20.	

(See Chapter 4 for more information about how this list is used.)

SUPER SECOND LIFE "OUT" LIST

What you want to exclude from your Super Second Life

Date:

1.	
2.	
3.	
4.	
5.	
6.	
7.	
8.	
9.	
10.	
11.	
12.	
13.	
14.	
15.	
16.	
17.	
18.	
19.	
20.	

(See Chapter 4 for more information about how this list is used.)

If this is a library book or is available for multiple or public use, do not write on this form. Please copy it first and write on your copy! Thank you.

MEDICAL HEALTH HISTORY QUESTIONNAIRE

NAME _____ Age _____ Today's Date _____

CURRENT MEDICAL PROBLEMS _____

_____

_____

OTHER CONCERNS you would like to discuss with the doctor _____

_____

List PRESCRIPTION MEDICINE you now take *(include dosage, reason you take it, who prescribed it)*:_____

_____

_____

_____

List OVER-THE-COUNTER MEDICINES, vitamins, and food supplements you take _____

_____

_____

ALLERGIES: _____ SENSITIVITIES _____

_____ _____

Do/did you EXERCISE? _____ How much? _____ hrs/wk, # of years? _____ Year you QUIT _____

Do/did you SMOKE? _____ How much? _____ packs/day _____ # of years _____ Year you QUIT

_____

Do/did you DRINK alcohol? _____ How much? _____ drinks/week _____ # of years _____

Year you QUIT _____ Previous or current problem with alcohol? _____ AA? _____

Do/did you use *(circle)*: caffeine   Nutrasweet   marijuana   cocaine   chewing tobacco   diet pills

Do you wear seat belts? _____ Do you wear sunscreen? _____ Ride a motorcycle/bicycle? _____

List SURGERIES you have had *(include year, surgeon, hospital)*: _____

_____

_____

_____

Describe HOSPITALIZATIONS/ILLNESSES not included above *(include year, hospital)*:

_____

_____

_____

_____

Have you had (circle):

migraines	hepatitis	mono	ulcer
bleeding problem	blood clots	head injury	drug addiction	gallstones
tuberculosis	STDs	seizures	memory trouble	arthritis
psoriasis	heart murmur	rheumatic fever	polio	shingles
alcoholism	depression	mental illness	gout	hemorrhoids
hearing trouble	vision trouble	other	_____	_____

WOMEN

Age at first period _____ Date of last normal period _____ # of pregnancies _____

# of live births _____ # of children living with you _____ birth control method _____

Date of last PAP _____ Done where _____

Date of last mammogram _____ Done where _____

Do you have (circle):

irregular periods	bad menstrual cramps	heavy periods	pelvic pain	infertility
female trouble	hot flashes	vaginal dryness	vaginal discharge	vaginal odor
vaginal itching	PMS	breast problems	abnormal mammogram	abnormal PAP smear

Medical Health History Questionnaire (2)

List diseases that run in your family _____

_____

Who in your FAMILY has/had *(circle if cause of death and write age of death)*

heart disease _____ genetic disorder _____

diabetes _____ cancer _____

thyroid disease _____ alcoholism _____

mental illness _____ arthritis _____

glaucoma _____ asthma _____

allergies _____ stomach problems _____

tuberculosis _____ high blood pressure _____

Who lives in your household? _____

Where do/did you work? _____

Describe your education/upbringing, etc. _____

How much do you weigh? _____ How much would you like to weigh? _____ Heaviest weight _____

When was your last:

tetanus shot _____ flu shot _____ EKG _____

TB test _____ HIV test _____ sigmoidoscopy _____

chest X-ray _____ pneumonia shot _____ hepatitis vaccine _____

rectal exam _____ blood test _____

Describe your diet: _____

_____

Describe your skin problems: _____

_____

Describe lung and breathing problems: _____

Describe problems with your stomach, intestines, colon, digestion, bowel movements: _____

_____

Describe any urinary trouble: _____

_____

Describe sexual concerns: _____

_____

Describe any bone, muscle, or joint problems: _____

_____

Describe any hormone problem: _____

_____

Describe any problems with your thinking, concentration, moods, energy level, interest in life, etc.: _____

_____

Describe problems with strength, sensation, coordination, neurologic function: _____

_____

Anything else? _____

_____

(See Chapter 6 for more information about how this questionnaire is used.)

Sight
hearing
smell
pain

Super Second Life Net Worth Worksheet: Year or Age— / Date:					
NET WORTH	Now	1 Year	5 Years	10 Years	15 Years
Assets					
Checking account(s)	$	$	$	$	$
Savings account(s)					
Bond(s)					
Certificate(s)					
Market value of home/apartment					
Market value of other real estate					
IRA and Keogh plans					
Cash value of life insurance					
Surrender value of annuities					
Equity in profit-sharing / pension plans					
Market value of stocks					
Market value of bonds					
Market value of mutual funds					
Current value of car(s)					
Current value of household furnishings and appliances					
Current value of furs and jewelry					
Loans receivable					
Other assets					
Total Assets (A)	$	$	$	$	$
Liabilities					
Mortgage balance	$	$	$	$	$
Loans: auto					
Loans: student					
Loans: home equity					
Current bills					
Credit-card balance					
Other debts:					
Total Liabilities (B)	$	$	$	$	$
Current Net Worth (A) minus (B)	$	$	$	$	$

(See Chapter 7 for more information about how this chart is used.)

Super Second Life Income Worksheet: Year or Age— / Date:					
INCOME	Annual	Monthly	Begins in Year	Ends in Year	Reserve
Social Security	$	$			$
Retirement benefits					
Disability benefits					
Survivor's benefits					
Pension plans					
Employer					
Voluntary (IRA, 401[k], Keogh)					
Veteran's benefits					
Interest					
Dividends					
Early retirement bonus					
Insurance payments					
Life insurance					
Health insurance					
Long-term care insurance					
Disability insurance					
Conversion of personal investments					
Retirement savings					
General savings					
Property and goods					
Mutual funds					
Treasury bills					
Stocks					
Bonds					
Certificates					
Annuities					
Loans receivable					
Inheritances					
After-death inheritance					
Living inheritance (cash gift transfers)					

INCOME (2)	Annual	Monthly	Begins in Year	Ends in Year	Reserve
Working Income	$	$			$
Full-time employment					
Part-time job:					
Part-time job:					
Self-employment income					
Residual income (royalties)					
In-kind income (companion, house tender)					
Home income					
Rental income					
Sale income					
Reverse mortgage					
Rental / sale of other real estate					
Gift income					
Personal holdings					
Sale of personal possessions					
Sale of collectibles					
Sale of car, boat, trailer, camper, etc.					
Other sales					
Use of emergency fund					
TOTAL INCOME	$	$			$

(See Chapter 7 for more information about how this chart is used.)

Super Second Life Expense Worksheet: Year or Age— / Date:					
EXPENSES	Annual	Monthly	Begins in Year	Ends in Year	Reserve
House payment or rent	$	$			$
Maintenance					
Furnishing					
Improvements					
Property tax					
Food					
Utilities					
Water					
Electricity					
Gas					
Oil					
Trash / Sewage					
Other:					
Inflation (2-3% a year)					
Phone					
Computer costs					
Clothing					
Purchases					
Cleaning					
Health costs					
Care					
Medicine					
Taxes					
Federal					
State					
Local					
Self-employment					
Transportation					
Car payments					
Gas, oil, repairs					
Parking					
Commuting / public transportation					
Professional fees					
Gifts and donations					
Loan repayments					

EXPENSES (2)	Annual	Monthly	Begins in Year	Ends in Year	Reserve
Loan debts	$	$			$
Personal care					
Care of family members or dependents					
Education					
Exercise / Fitness					
Travel / Vacation					
Savings investment					
Emergency fund					
Hobby costs					
Pets					
Entertainment					
Divorce costs (alimony, child support)					
Interest: credit card and other					
Assumed debts: children/others					
Insurance					
Health					
Auto					
Property					
Life					
Disability					
Liability					
TOTAL EXPENSES	$	$			$

(See Chapter 7 for more information about how this chart is used.)

Super Second Life Money Worksheet: Year or Age / Date:		
Annual basic living expenses		(A) $
Annual basic income:		
Annual Social Security income	$	
Annual pension income	$	
Other annual income: Royalties	$	
Other annual income:	$	
Other annual income:	$	
Total income	(add totals above)	(B) $
Annual basic income deficit/surplus	(A) - (B)	(C) $
Monthly supplemental income needed	÷12	$
Special super life expenses this year	(from Action Plan)	(D) $
Total money desired for this year	(A) + (D)	$
Maximum income deficit/surplus	if C is -, (C) + (D) if C is +, (C) - (D)	(E) $
Monthly supplemental income needed	÷12	$
Additional income source(s)	Amount	
Income source:	$	
Income source:	$	
Income source:	$	
Income source:	$	
Income source:	$	
Income source:	$	
Additional income available this year	$	(F)
Total income deficit/surplus for this year	C + F	$

(See Chapters 7 and 14 for more information about how this chart is used.)

SUPER SECOND LIFE DREAM LIST

NAME _____ Date _____

DREAMS
1.
2.
3.
4.
5.
6.
7.
8.
9.
10.
11.
12.
13.
14.
15.
16.
17.
18.
19.
20.
21.
22.
23.
24.
25.
26.
27.
28.

(See Chapter 8 for more information about how this list is used.)

TIME-PEG #1—MIDDLE YEARS (-) / Date:
1.
2.
3.
4.
5.
6.
7.
8.
10.
11.
12.
13.
14.
15.
16.
17.
18.
19.
20.
21.
22.
23.
24.
25.
26.
27.
28.

(See Chapter 9 for more information about how this list is used.)

If this is a library book or is available for multiple or public use, do <u>not</u> write on this form. Please copy it first and write on your copy! Thank you.

TIME-PEG #2—EARLY DISCERNING YEARS (-) / Date:
1.
2.
3.
4.
5.
6.
7.
8.
9.
10.
11.
12.
13.
14.
15.
16.
17.
18.
19.
20.
21.
22.
23.
24.
25.
26.
27.
28.

(See Chapter 9 for more information about how this list is used.)

TIME-PEG #3—LATER DISCERNING YEARS (-   ) / Date:
1.
2.
3.
4.
5.
6.
7.
8.
9.
10.
11.
12.
13.
14.
15.
16.
17.
18.
19.
20.
21.
22.
23.
24.
25.
26.
27.
28.

(See Chapter 9 for more information about how this list is used.)

If this is a library book or is available for multiple or public use, do not write on this form. Please copy it first and write on your copy! Thank you.

	TIME-PEG #4—REFLECTIVE YEARS (+) / Date:
1.	
2.	
3.	
4.	
5.	
6.	
7.	
8.	
9.	
10.	
11.	
12.	
13.	
14.	
15.	
16.	
17.	
18.	
19.	
20.	
21.	
22.	
23.	
24.	
25.	
26.	

(See Chapter 9 for more information about how this list is used.)

PERSONAL DREAM LIST / Date:	

(See Chapter 11 for more information about how this list is used.)

If this is a library book or is available for multiple or public use, do not write on this form. Please copy it first and write on your copy! Thank you.

OVERLAPPING OR SHARED DREAM LIST / Date:	

(See Chapter 11 for more information about how this list is used.)

If this is a library book or is available for multiple or public use, do not write on this form. Please copy it first and write on your copy! Thank you.

ACTION STEP WORKSHEET / Date:	
Name:	
Dream:	$
Action Steps : [Who, what, why, where, when, and how?]	

(See Chapter 12 for more information about how this form is used.)

FINANCIAL WORKSHEET / Date:		
Name:		
Dream:	COSTS	POTENTIAL INCOME
	$	$
	$	$

(See Chapter 13 for more information about how this chart used.)

If this is a library book or is available for multiple or public use, do <u>not</u> write on this form. Please copy it first and write on your copy! Thank you.

JOINED ACTION STEP WORKSHEET / Date:	
Names:	
Joined Dream:	$

(See Chapter 13 for more information about how this chart is used.)

If this is a library book or is available for multiple or public use, do not write on this form. Please copy it first and write on your copy! Thank you.

FINAL ACTION PLAN / Time Peg - / Date:

Name:

Dream:	**$**

ACTION STEPS

FINANCIAL CALCULATIONS	COSTS	POTENTIAL INCOME
	$	$
TOTALS	$	$

HEALTH CONSIDERATIONS

PREPARATORY ACTIONS

(See Chapter 14 for more information about how this form is used.)

CO-FUNDED BUDGET SHEET TIME-PEG ( ): Years - / Date:			
Co-Funded Dreams:			
TOTALS	$	$	$

(See Chapter 14 for more information about how this form is used.)

If this is a library book or is available for multiple or public use, do not write on this form. Please copy it first and write on your copy! Thank you.

PERSONAL BUDGET SHEET TIME-PEG ( ): Years - / Date:			
Dreams:			
Funds available after co-funded expenses are deducted	$	$	$
	$	$	$
TOTALS	$	$	$

(See Chapter 14 for more information about how this form is used.)

ANNUAL ACTION RECORD SHEET / Date:	
Name:	

Dream:	**Year:**

Actions taken:	Actual cost/income:

Changes made this year:	Changes suggested for the future:

(See Chapter 14 for more information about how this form is used.)

CONFLICT RESOLUTION SHEET / Date:		
"What I want..."	"The Gap of Resolution"	"What I have..."

(See Chapter 15 for more information about how this form is used.)

If this is a library book or is available for multiple or public use, do <u>not</u> write on this form. Please copy it first and write on your copy! Thank you.

SUPER SECOND LIFE PROCESS CHECK-OFF CHART / Date:		
Chapter / Item	Progress Notes	Done!
2	Me Now List #1		
2	Me Now List #2		
2	Me Now List #3		
2	Me Now List #4		
2	Me Now List #5		
4	Super Second Life "In" List		
4	Super Second Life "Out" List		
6	Medical Health History Questionnaire		
7	Super Second Life Net Worth Worksheet		
7	Super Second Life Income Worksheet		
7	Super Second Life Expense Worksheet		
7	Super Second Life Money Worksheet		
8	Super Second Life Dream List		
9	Time-Pegs		
10	Commitment		
11	Personal Dream List		
11	Overlapping or Shared Dream List		
12	Action Step Worksheet		
13	Action Step Worksheet		
13	Joined Action Step Worksheet		
14	Final Action Plan		
14	Personal Budget Sheet		
14	Co-Funded Budget Sheet		
14	Annual Action Record Sheet		

(See Chapter 16 for more information about how this form is used.)

INDEX

ORDER FORM

◆   ◆

FAX   Fax orders: **(805) 937-3035**. Include this form please.

☎   Telephone: Call **1 (800) 563-1454** toll free. Please have your credit card ready.

💻   E-mail: **order@agemasters.com**

✉   Postal: Agemasters, P.O. Box 6405, Santa Maria, CA 93456.

Please send the following books, disks, cassettes, or reports. I understand that I may return any of them within 30 days for a full refund (less shipping)—for any reason, no questions asked.

_____

_____

_____

_____

_____

_____

For disks, please indicate: IBM/compatible [   ]   Macintosh [   ]

For further information about our products, please check www.agemasters.com and www.sops.com.

[   ] Please send more information about Gordon Burgett speaking to our group or organization.
     Name of organization _____

Name _____

Address _____

City _____ State _____ ZIP _____

Telephone _____ E-mail _____

Sales tax: Please add 7.75% for products shipped to California addresses.

Shipping: <u>U.S.</u>, Please add $4 for first book or disk, $2 for each additional. We ship PRIORITY mail. <u>International</u>, please contact us for type of shipping and cost.

Payment: [   ] Check   [   ] VISA   [   ] Mastercard

Card number: _____ Expires _____

     Name on card _____

(Please copy this form, complete it, and submit it with each order.)

◆ OTHER BURGETT PRODUCTS ◆

(All products are shipped the day the order is received.)

<u>Additional copies</u> of ***How to Create Your Own Super Second Life.*** A great gift for any friend eager to make full use of the last 30 years! — $19.95 (3 books, $54, save $5.85)

<u>Make your own lists, forms, and worksheets!</u> Now available: *every* list, form, and worksheet (plus the rest of the Appendix) in ***How to Create Your Own Super Second Life,*** on IBM or Mac disk. All 28, to modify, use as is, or reproduce for as long as you wish!—$15

◆ *More information? See www.agemasters.com for the items above; www.sops.com for those below!* ◆

<u>Gordon Burgett's funniest book:</u> ***Treasure and Scavenger Hunts.*** The best of the past! This 128-page book shows how to design, plan, then throw a super party built around a combination treasure/scavenger hunt. For adults, but all can join in! You'll be a genius.—$ 9.95.

<u>Want to write for publication during your Super Second Life?</u> Then you're entering Burgett's arena. Two of his books are particularly helpful putting you in print and fattening your coffers: ***How to Sell and Resell Your Magazine Articles***, a recent Writer's Digest Book Club top choice (240 pages, $17.99), and his travel writing top seller, ***The Travel Writer's Guide*** (320 pages, $14.95). Plus an annual report, "*100 Best U.S. Newspaper Travel Markets*," in report form or on disk (IBM or Mac), $10.

<u>Are you a font of valuable niche information?</u> A great way to sell back what you know during your later years! By good fortune, Gordon wrote the three key books in this field: ***Empire-Building by Writing and Speaking*** ($12.95), ***Niche Marketing*** ($14.95), and ***Publishing to Niche Markets*** ($14.95)—all three for $35 (save $7.85). No area is riper for profit or easier to tap for a seasoned veteran.

<u>Rather hear a super seminar, with the same in-class workbook?</u> Gordon Burgett has delighted audiences with his straightforward, fun, easy-to-do presentations more than 1,000 times since 1980. The programs are now available, produced in studio on audio cassettes and sold at the cost of admission! "**How to Sell 75% of Your Travel Writing**" combines the best of his two top programs and "**How to Publish Your Own Book and Earn $50,000 Profit!**" explains the niche publishing bonanza—each two hours long and $29.95—while "**How to Set Up and Market Your Own Seminar**" ($44.95/3 hours) and "**Producing and Selling Your Own Audio Cassettes**" ($9.95/1 hour) also open up new, second life fun doors.

(To order, please copy and submit the ORDER FORM on the back of this page.)